THE
LAST BOYS
PICKED

Helping Boys Who
Don't Play Sports Survive
Bullies and Boyhood

JANET SASSON EDGETTE with **BETH MARGOLIS RUPP**

BERKLEY BOOKS, NEW YORK

BERKLEY BOOKS
Published by the Penguin Group
Penguin Group (USA) Inc.
375 Hudson Street, New York, New York 10014, USA
Penguin Group (Canada), 90 Eglinton Avenue East, Suite 700, Toronto, Ontario M4P 2Y3, Canada
(a division of Pearson Penguin Canada Inc.) • Penguin Books Ltd., 80 Strand, London WC2R 0RL,
England • Penguin Group Ireland, 25 St. Stephen's Green, Dublin 2, Ireland (a division of Penguin
Books Ltd.) • Penguin Group (Australia), 250 Camberwell Road, Camberwell, Victoria 3124, Australia
(a division of Pearson Australia Group Pty. Ltd.) • Penguin Books India Pvt. Ltd., 11 Community
Centre, Panchsheel Park, New Delhi—110 017, India • Penguin Group (NZ), 67 Apollo Drive,
Rosedale, Auckland 0632, New Zealand (a division of Pearson New Zealand Ltd.) • Penguin Books
(South Africa) (Pty.) Ltd., 24 Sturdee Avenue, Rosebank, Johannesburg 2196, South Africa

Penguin Books Ltd., Registered Offices: 80 Strand, London WC2R 0RL, England

While the author has made every effort to provide accurate Internet addresses and telephone numbers at
the time of publication, neither the author nor the publisher assumes any responsibility for errors, or for
changes that occur after publication. Further, the publisher does not have any control over and does not
assume any responsibility for author or third-party websites or their content.

This book is an original publication of The Berkley Publishing Group.

PUBLISHING HISTORY
Berkley trade paperback edition / September 2012

Library of Congress Cataloging-in-Publication Data

Edgette, Janet Sasson.
The last boys picked / Janet Sasson Edgette ; with Beth Margolis Rupp.
p.   cm.
ISBN 978-0-425-24543-9
1. Sports—Psychological aspects.   2. Boys—Psychology.   3. Masculinity.
4. Sports for children—Psychological aspects.   5. Physical education for children—Psychological
aspects.   6. Athletic ability—Psychological aspects.   I. Rupp, Beth Margolis.   II. Title.
GV706.4.E34   2012
796.01—dc23
2011050914

PRINTED IN THE UNITED STATES OF AMERICA

10   9   8   7   6   5   4   3   2   1

"An important and relevant addition to the parenting bookshelf. It offers insightful and practical advice for helping all boys—those who don't play sports as well as those who do—navigate the sometimes difficult journey of boyhood."

—Michael Gurian, author of *The Wonder of Boys*

"Clear, well-written and engaging . . . Essential reading for everyone who works with, lives with, or cares about boys who do not fit the stereotype of 'masculinity.'"

—Linda Knauss, assistant professor of clinical psychology,
Widener University

"*The Last Boys Picked* is rich with illuminating case examples and practical advice that will be of inestimable value to mothers and fathers . . . Sasson Edgette and Margolis Rupp have helped to lay the groundwork not only for improved family life, but for a society that can and must become more responsive to and respectful of the unique attributes of children and adults of both genders."

—Dr. Brad Sachs, psychologist and author of *The Good
Enough Child* and *The Good Enough Teen*

"A thoughtful and helpful guide to steering boys through a world that often values prowess with a ball and bat more than thoughtfulness, kindness, and intellect. Here is the balance and wisdom parents need."
—Rabbi David Wolpe

"Meaningful guidance on how we adults can be more thoughtful in our behavior and in our conversations with all children. It is a great book with practical approaches for improving the arenas—sporting and non-sporting—in which children play and assisting them in growing up with both a strong sense of worth and fairness."

—Billy Cunningham, NBA All-Star and coach

"A well-researched, yet practically grounded book that offers academics, parents, and educators insights and strategies into helping to understand and cater to boys who are not overly interested in sports. It fills a much needed gap in the literature on boys and schooling."

—Dr. Natasha Ridge, executive director, Sheikh Saud Bin Saqr Al

"A vital resource for building inclusion, compassion, confidence, and humanity in every child's life . . . I will return to this book again and again and don't know a single family or school that couldn't use it."   —Homa S. Tavangar, author of *Growing Up Global*

"Full of real-life stories and everyday solutions as well as remarkable thought leadership, [*The Last Boys Picked*] demonstrates how to engender all children with nonconformist, nonaggressive values that support relationships, creativity, introspection, well-being, compassion, justice, and an expanded concept of success."

—Dr. Joni Carley, Leadership Edge Consulting & Coaching

"A powerful reflection on the pernicious personal, social, and political consequences of a constricted construction of masculinity in a world that cries out for new definition."

—James Jerry Clark, academic research and communications specialist, American Reading Company

"Filled with practical information and ideas, this book can be a vital resource for school and mental health professionals, as well as parents and caretakers."

—John McCarthy, director, Center for Counselor Training and Services, Indiana University of Pennsylvania

"A must-read for all parents, educators, counselors, and coaches . . . It is our responsibility as adults to start the process of changing society's outdated view that all boys should be coerced into athletic interests and team sports. What better way to start his process than by reading *The Last Boys Picked*?"

—Gary McClurg, teacher, guidance counselor, coach

AUSTIN AND JAKE

Two months before my brother passed away from liver cancer, he invited me out to dinner. I don't remember Phil and me ever going out to eat before like that, just ourselves. I told him about this book I was writing—about boys who aren't so into sports and all—and he abruptly put down his fork and threw his head back, blindsided by memories. Seemingly out of nowhere, Phil began telling me about his memories of our mother watching the tennis matches at Wimbledon every summer:

"She watched only the men," he said, sharing with me the fixed image he had of her even after forty years: Mom with her coffee cup suspended in midair, her mouth agape. "I asked her once why she was so fascinated with tennis players," my brother said. "'Because they're athletes!' she exclaimed. "As if this was supposed to be an obvious thing to me, her son, who loved music and science and whose closest connection to base-ball was my kick-ass baseball-card collection."

—*Janet Sasson Edgette*

.   .   .

To my husband, my partner,
a good and fair man, the love of my life.
—*Beth Margolis Rupp*

CONTENTS

AUTHORS' NOTES

I was in my study facing away from the door when Jake, my nine-year-old son, walked in.

"Mom, what are you doing?" he asked.

I swiveled around in my chair and answered, "Thinking about writing a new book."

"About what?"

"About boys who don't like sports."

"Oh," he said, pausing, and then, "like me!"

"Yes, like you," I replied, relieved by his favorable reaction. Jake's story is central to the book, even though it plays in the background. Without him onboard, I wouldn't have been able to tell it.

"Well," Jake made a point to add, before leaving me to my project, "you better hurry up and write that book!"

Better than relieved, now I was inspired. I got busy writing, and stayed that way for the next seven years.

The Last Boys Picked is all about boys like Jake who don't enjoy a lot of the physical activities that other boys their ages do. Sometimes it's because they're not good at sports or they find them boring. Sometimes it's because their natures or personalities better suit other kinds of activities. To complicate matters, they may have trouble finding other boys who share similar interests and are occasionally, and almost always erroneously, subject to suspicions about their sexuality. These boys are often pushed to play sports or join sports teams, despite their objections or obvious discomfort. Their genuine aptitudes often go unrecognized, and they are rarely part of the popular crowd. With their less fashionable and less physically vigorous interests, they are poised to be marginalized by their own peer group. In the end, there's just no being smart enough or good enough at anything else to keep these boys out of that small pool of kids left for last on the gym floor when playing teams are chosen.

The American masculine ideal has always been one of a rather fearless, independent, no-holds-barred kind of guy. Conceived surely out of that frontier spirit with which historians and novelists and romantics imbue our early pioneers, this model for males has served to shape everything from our advertising icons (the Marlboro Man) to our movie stars (John Wayne, Al Pacino, Bruce Willis) to our comic book heroes (Superman, Iron Man). It's no wonder then, really, that the *non*physical skills of boys and men in this country are more background material than foreground, the ones guys discount when jockeying among themselves for position. It's bigger than just a "guy thing," though; our society at large places this same premium on physical aptitudes when appraising its males in all kinds of settings, at the inadvertent but overlooked expense of millions of boys whose interests and talents lean toward the linguistic, spatial, musical, or interpersonal, rather than kinesthetic.

For someone like me who is both a psychologist for children and teenagers, and the parent of a boy who doesn't play sports, it's surprising and disturbing that this entire subject matter has gone unexamined and unchallenged for so long. There is chatter about it here and there—a few books, and an occasional article or blog referencing the challenges faced by what are typically termed "nonathletic" boys, or, as Ken Corbett, author of *Boyhoods: Rethinking Masculinities*, artfully says, "the boys who are not in the park." But there is little written on how to help these boys, and no call to action. It struck me as particularly ironic that on the heels of the Boys' Movement, which pointed out a need to release American boys from our culture's constricting definition of masculinity, there had been such little consideration of the population of boys who are socially penalized for not being "male enough." After years of hovering quietly over our collective consciousness, this issue of how we treat boys and men who don't conform to traditional masculine ideals is due for landing.

It was a natural step to invite my friend and colleague, Beth Margolis Rupp, to join me on this project. The mother of three boys herself, and an educator who for years and in a variety of settings championed youth leadership development through civic engagement and community service, Beth brought a perspective that included among a child's natural resources his or her larger community of family, mentors, counselors, coaches, teachers, religious leaders, community youth leaders, recreational planners, curriculum developers, and camp directors, and all of their respective institutions. Together, Beth and I recognized the limitations of classical therapy, with its private conversations and off-site location, as the answer to helping non-sports-oriented boys grow up soundly in a culture that prizes physical prowess and a macho demeanor. We focus instead on the rich social networks that make up a child's different communities, seeing them as having both the authority and the opportunity to affirm the masculinity, personal worth, and social credibility of these often underappreciated boys.

It was Beth who said to me that our society makes kings out of certain types of boys, and that we all know who they are. They're the ones who are big and strong, confident and daring. We count on them to entertain us with their physicality, and do battle for us when we need them to. From the start, these types of boys have been our standard-bearers for all things masculine, an unfortunate anointing. A few of these boys (and men) play out the role honorably, but many don't, and instead become bullies and opportunists who understand that kings don't really have to follow the rules.

This we can change, however. As adults, we are responsible for correcting the inequitable balances of power that we observe among children, and as a part of that we need to state more loudly and more clearly that the exclusion of certain children by others is not okay. Because by not intervening where we can—in the micro of the corner of a classroom where four cheeky boys surround a fifth, and in the macro of institutions whose policies continue to discriminate against boys who stray from the norm—we are in effect endorsing this junior monarchy in which the boys with brawn rule.

Children need both to know and to feel that they have some measurable degree of personal power. I'll never forget the experience of sitting in my office with Marie, eighteen years old and a freshman in college. Marie had been a therapy client of mine the year before, during her senior year of high school. In town on one of her breaks, she made an appointment to come in for a follow-up visit.

Marie had enjoyed an active social life in high school, keeping the same group of friends throughout her four years. Never one to make waves, she fell into a pattern of simply going along with whatever her friends chose to do. Easily exploited for her agreeable and generous nature, however, Marie became to go-to girl for anyone needing a ride or cigarette money or a sympathetic ear. In all the months I saw Marie, I don't recall ever hearing about a time when she stood up and said, "You know, guys, what I want matters, too."

But sitting with Marie now was a whole different story. She filled the room with her presence, and captivated me with her stories about adjusting to college. At some point I told Marie how compelling I found her company. She nodded her head quickly and smiled at me with her eyes; she knew. "Something's changed for you," I said. "What is it?"

"I discovered that I have *agency*," said Marie. "Being away at school, on my own, I had to do things for myself, including advocate for myself. So I developed a voice. And people listened to it. I found out that if I didn't like something, I could do something to change it—most of the time anyway. I discovered that what I thought and what I said mattered, and, Dr. Edgette, it was huge."

Agency. The power to influence others, to change things, *to make something stop.* It *is* huge, and all children should have at least enough of it to be able to protect themselves against exploitation by other children or by adults. But we're not there yet, or anywhere close. I worry that, in the same way some parents allow themselves to feel reassured by the news that their teenager is ("at least") not on drugs or in trouble with the law, the American community of adults, horrified by journalists' and authors' accounts of child slavery, child prostitution, and child soldiery, has become complacent about the status of children's rights here in our own country.

There are still millions of kids in this country who are not free to learn multiplication or make new friends or walk to school without having to fear being victimized by some other child's unsated appetite for violence or emotional torment. As parents and teachers and guardians of youth, we fail boys in our duty to protect whenever we dismiss these particularly mean or excluding behaviors as "boys being boys." And I mean we fail *all* the boys—the ones who make up the inner circle as much as the ones who don't. We fail them by virtue of passing on the opportunity to shape the social culture into a more respectful and humane form, as it manifests right under our noses. That's exactly why Beth and I say that this topic of how we treat boys who don't like to play sports is really much bigger than it might appear. Many people don't see that it's not "just" about those boys; it's about all of us. Maybe that's why it hasn't gotten the attention it should have received by now. People tend to notice problems that make a lot of noise, and this one doesn't.

So maybe that should be our starting point—helping these boys to make more noise. We can do that. We can help them insist that what they think and what they want to say, what they do, and who they are, matter very much. We can't be everywhere all the time to intervene on their behalf, and kids do better when defended by their own voice anyway. We can also make more noise ourselves, in the process of connecting with others who similarly appreciate all the different ways in which a guy can be a guy. And there's one other thing we can do to help: We can make a point of recognizing and applauding the boys and men whose elegant socialization reveals its success less in their having become better males than in their having become better human beings. In a real democracy, there may be no kings and no queens, but there still are plenty of places for a boy to be a prince.

Janet Sasson Edgette
Exton, Pennsylvania

. . .

Without realizing, we have witnessed and accepted the marginalization of boys by boys as a norm. Perhaps as adults we are immune, or have developed amnesia to the situation played out all over in our communities. Many boys and young adults quietly suffer, not even having a name for the pain. In our schools, communities, playgrounds and even in our homes, we, as a society, have unwittingly perpetuated the acceptance of rude, unkind, and sometimes brutal behavior from our boys. By saying and doing little or nothing, we teach tolerance for the wrong behaviors. Through our collective silence we have condoned bullying, which has resulted in the decay of innocence and loss of character. This decade is a turning point as we experience increased violence and suicide. We can no longer tolerate the systemic exclusion of anyone.

Over the past twenty-five years, my professional focus has been in developing constructs in support of the socially responsible individual/citizen. Experience with private and public schools, faith-based communities, community-based organizations, and governmental agencies has given me a deep understanding and appreciation of the varying needs of individuals within society. Working with many thousands of students and teachers who have heeded the call to civic engagement, leadership, and social improvement has provided me with an optimistic perspective on youth. Utilizing community-based service learning methodology as the best practice in character, leadership, and citizenship education, I have helped to create tools that engage students in a combination of learning and action that encourages intellectual, social, emotional, spiritual, and physical development. According to Eugene C. Roehlkepartain, acting president and CEO of the Search Institute, "They learn that they can make a real impact on resolving social challenges, problems, and needs. Also, they experience enhanced problem-solving skills and develop greater planning abilities; as well as enhanced civic engagement attitudes, skills, and behaviors. A new generation of caring and experienced citizens, activists, and volunteers is cultivated." This approach to teaching and community building has become a framework for strengthening the individual and society.

As a mother of three boys, I have learned from my children to empower each boy to excel and contribute from their strengths. My first son, Zander, was not an athlete. He was and is an outdoorsman, happiest when covered in mud, digging for frogs and snakes. His greatest strength is his passion for the environment and he recently graduated university with a degree in art and environmental studies. Nathan is an all-around athlete—lean, strong, and active. He played U8 and U9 community travel soccer and was the goalie. In 2000, he was never scored on—a shutout year in the net. The pressure to win from the team and, most of all, from the coach provided a level of intensity that broke his desire to compete. He stopped playing soccer at the end of the season. Through high school he played on the school teams and was even a captain. He played for fun, competition, the camaraderie, and the exercise. He even liked the laps. He never wanted or needed to win again. Ethan was born ten years after Nathan. He is now eleven years old and growing up in Abu Dhabi, United

Arab Emirates, learning about being a global citizen. He loves to play football (aka soccer in the United States) and win. He also sings in the school choir and made the school musical. Each boy is profoundly different, and profoundly similar, sharing a core set of values.

My husband, who is an architect, provided our sons the early childhood experiences of working alongside him and learning to build furniture, repair roofs, doors, and windows, and paint. Participating with their father helped them bond to him and to each other while learning new life skills. Establishing family rituals, camping, caring for pets, and chores have helped to solidify and engage us as a working family that lives and celebrates their talents and values.

Each of us can individually affect those boys closest to us but we must do more. This book is an opportunity for me to play a role in changing the rules, the referees, the audience, and the game as a whole, to create a level playing field to ensure all boys can play as champions. Some boys overcome, some minimally adapt to the unbearable, but they can find themselves able to tackle new situations with grace and courage. I suspect this comes from self-knowledge and a deep sense of self-worth thanks to a caring friend, adult, or simply their own resilience and emotional intelligence. However, some boys lack the internal skills or safety nets and become targets for abuse and self-abuse. Until there is a shift in how we define play, winning, success, and competition, there will be a profound cost to the boys, the community, and the society.

Collaborating on this book gave me a place to contribute my

voice as a mother and as an educator concerned about raising children for a civil society.

Along with Janet, I have examined the many conversations, narratives, and undeclared policies on boys in our lives. It is my sincere belief that the roles we play as parents, educators, therapists, and coaches will shape future citizenship and our communities. I am invested in the making; this book is a call to action, to reframe the experience of growing up male. Coauthoring this book gave me an opportunity to shout out about the pain of witnessing the loss of boys to bullying and contribute to the field of raising gentlemen.

I am honored to work with Dr. Janet Edgette and contribute to the lives of our readers.

Beth Margolis Rupp
Abu Dhabi, United Arab Emirates

CHAPTER ONE

Living in Dread of Phys Ed

Jake is my light-framed, animal-loving, ten-year-old son and he doesn't care much for contact sports. I saw him looking a little glum one day after school, so I asked him if something was the matter.

"We played kickball today at recess," Jake replied. I asked him how it went.

"Well, everyone got mad at me because I missed the ball when Ryan kicked it to me."

I could see it all clearly in my mind, but the only thing I could think of to say was, "Oh."

Jake continued. "They made me team captain."

"Really?" I wondered out loud. I was suspicious.

"Really. But I think they were just messing around because whenever I picked someone to be on my team, he'd say he wasn't playing anymore, and then the other captain would pick the same kid and he'd say he was playing. I didn't have anyone on my team, so I just went back inside." My suspicions were founded.

Later on, around ten-thirty that night, I noticed Jake lying awake in his bed. We'd said good night over an hour before.

"Can't sleep?" I asked.

"No," he replied.

"Still thinking about the kickball game?"

"Yup. I want to go to sleep but I just keep thinking about it and wishing I'd caught that ball."

"What do you think would have happened if you had caught it?"

"I think maybe some of them would have wanted to be on my team the next time I picked them."

I smiled softly and let it go. Soon enough Jake would learn that he could have caught that ball one hundred times over and it still wouldn't have changed the playground politics.

"Hey, you know what?" I said brightly. "I think this is the perfect time to do the read-something-boring-in-bed-and-see-what-happens routine."

My son shot up in bed with an enormous smile on his face. "I know!" he called out. "I'll look around for a *Sports Illustrated for Kids*—that'll put me right to sleep!"

How I laughed: a boy's perfect private revenge.

Of my three boys, two are twins. One of the twins, Austin, strapping and agile, is an exceptional athlete. Jake is the other twin.

With his lankier frame and noncompetitive nature, he is more at home draped over the family dog than fielding fly balls. Jake isn't particularly fast, and his hand-eye coordination is so-so. He likes to bike, hike, and swim, but avoids contact sports, high-risk activities, and anything involving a team. Austin and Jake are very close as brothers and spend a lot of time together at home, but outside of the home, they inhabit totally different worlds.

Big, strong, athletically gifted boys have always dominated childhood's social landscape. Their physical presence alone trumps the clout of smaller, quieter boys, but it's their love of sports and fierce desire to win anything and everything that really jettisons these boys to the top—especially in America, home of the Marlboro Man and seven-figure pro athlete salaries, and where it is assumed that being faster, stronger, louder, or mightier is always going to be better.

And then there are other boys, the boys about whom this book was written. These boys don't match up very evenly with the standard-issue high-octane, sports-loving, risk-taking, heat-seeking missile of a kid most people in this country think of when they think of boys. Some of them have learned that they can create more magic with their imaginations than with their feet. Some simply eschew competition and other divisive activities in favor of ones that bring people together, showcasing empathetic and other nuanced interpersonal skills not typically seen until later adolescence or adulthood. Other boys in this group may love competing but find that their hand-eye coordination or visual-spatial processing skills aren't very good, so they creatively and adaptively channel their competitive drive elsewhere—biking the farthest, having more songs on their iPod than anyone else, knowing obscure breeds of dogs.

There are, of course, all the boys in between the ones described above, variously parked toward one end or the other of the sliding scale of gender-normative behavior that, for the conversation at hand, we're calling play. And also, lots of boys with feet in both camps, for no other reason than that they like a broad range of activities, some sports-oriented and some not. Beth's middle son, Nathan, is one of these: He played the lead in his school musical, founded the school's literary magazine, and was cocaptain of its lacrosse team. Earlier, in primary school, he'd trained to be a peer mediator. Nathan wasn't trying to be some kind of Renaissance kid; he just loved doing those things and he did them well. It is easier for some children than others, though; confidence, vitality, a broad and recognizable skill set, and opportunity play crucial roles. So do the educational institutions that kids attend. A Quaker school taught Nathan to mediate, and the play and magazine and lacrosse all took place on the grounds of a small private Waldorf school, one of an association of independent schools providing students with interdisciplinary, experiential learning opportunities that take into account children's intellectual, practical, and spiritual development. Both Nathan and his schools are anomalies.

As a rule, in our nation's culture, a boy's nonconformance with schoolyard measures of masculinity will, early and quickly, set him sharply apart from the other boys on the block.

He won't be the only one affected either. Parents often suffer a bewildering helplessness that comes from seeing their child struggle socially and not knowing what to do about it. If they try to force their son to become involved in sports, they risk bringing the problem home. All that happens then is that boys, who while at home might have felt safe from the pressures of having to be athletic, are now at risk for feeling pressured around the clock, and by the people they want least of all to disappoint.

Neither are siblings immune to the emotional impact that chronic teasing or excluding can have on a brother. I had to work pretty hard to free Austin from a self-imposed responsibility he felt to protect Jake from the pranks and taunts of opportunistic schoolmates. I've seen siblings take the opposite approach, too. Finding it easier to blame the victim than stand and defend him, athletic brothers of non-athletic boys will in such cases join the ranks of all the other kids and occasional adults who wonder out loud, "What the heck is the matter with this kid who doesn't like a good game of one-on-one?"

> "If you were going to be picked last you were better off not even showing up."
>
> Henry Dunow, *The Way Home: Scenes from a Season, Lessons from a Lifetime*

The Last Boys Picked

In the interminable moments before his name is begrudgingly called, the last boy picked for kickball or flag football is getting a life lesson in what it means to be considered a liability. For anyone who remembers elementary school phys ed and its unleg-islated twin, recess, it's a familiar memory. If you happen to have been one of the boys left for last, it's also a painful one. Alternat-ing turns, the team captains—boys chosen for their athletic prowess or popularity or both—pick from among the rest of the bunch their next team player. Eventually, there are only three or four boys left. Then there's just one.

"I was one of those kids picked only at the very end," recalled Alan, an optometrist in his midfifties who grew up small for his age. "I spent elementary school and junior high feeling like there was this club and I was never going to be a part of it. I couldn't keep up with certain things, like rope climbing in gym. I just didn't have the arm strength. It was embarrassing. Plus, I wasn't as developed as the other kids, and there's no way to hide that when everyone is undressing in the locker room. Everybody looks. Everybody notices. You can't hide it, it's out there."

I asked Alan what he wanted this book to accomplish. "What I would want this book to do," he replied, taking his time to consider the question, "is to let these boys know that they are not alone, and that there are other things they'll find they're good at that matter at least as much as how high you can climb or how good you are at the foul line." Alan gazed absently for a moment before quickly adding, "And that life gets better. Mainly, that life really does get better when you get older."

Even without the unwitting assistance of teachers and coaches whose means for putting together sports teams included this cruel schoolyard draft, grade-school-age boys and girls have always managed, silently but unmistakably, to establish their own social order based on a number of factors, one of them being physical aptitude. It took Boys' Movement authors Dan Kindlon and Michael Thompson to say what kids in schools have known all along: that the coolness factor associated with being athletic has created a veritable caste system. In their book, *Raising Cain: Protecting the Emotional Life of Boys*, Kindlon and Thompson note that even in its mildest form, this system leaves nonathletic boys feeling undervalued. At its worst, they add, it means that the "biggest, strongest boys make lower-status boys suffer. And not only do unathletic boys suffer socially, they often watch from the sidelines as the star athletes win the hearts of the most popular girls at school." The authors furthermore state that although our culture pays a lot of lip service to supporting the idea of sensitive males, "stereotyped images of masculinity are still with us . . . Neanderthal professional wrestlers; hockey "goons," ready at the slightest provocation to drop their sticks and pummel an opponent; multimillionaire professional athletes in trouble with the law . . . angry, drug-using, misogynist rock stars." Seems to us there's more work to do.

> "Being up at bat was a horrible experience. My standards for a tolerable Saturday morning dropped over the course of a season. At first I thought, if I just got a few hits in each practice or game, and didn't strike out too many times, it'd be okay. But by the end of the season, I wanted only to not be the worst player. I could deal with being the third worst or even second worst. But I remember praying every Saturday morning, "Oh please, God, please don't let me be the worst."
>
> Alan

Bad Boys Rule

"We parents like to believe that our sons really do enjoy getting sweaters for Christmas and that they'll floss every day at summer camp," says columnist Amy Dickinson in her January 31, 2000, *Time* article about the social regard boys get from being tough. But truthfully, Dickinson acknowledges, "in the real world, kids, like adults, are impressed by power." And power, she adds, doesn't always come in savory packages.

Who are the popular boys in grade school? Dickinson points out a study published in the *Journal of Developmental Psychology* that looked at 452 boys from a variety of backgrounds.[1] Many of the boys who were granted high social status by their classmates were smart, cool, athletic, and respectful. No surprises there. But a third of the boys who were considered popular, and who were held in higher regard, were kids considered to be "extremely antisocial"—tough kids who were mediocre students and who fought and dominated the classroom. Aggression, noted lead researcher Philip Rodkin, can make kids powerful and popular at young ages. But I wonder if it is the aggression per se that influences their popularity, or its contribution to a child's athleticism and competitiveness, traits that are more easily understood as appealing? It's not clear. There's the other possibility, too, that the "popularity" of some of these aggressive, antisocial kids is really a function of feigned approval and superficial compliance on the parts of schoolmates looking to stay out of their line of fire.

A different study, conducted in Canada,[2] also examined this connection between athletic skills and social acceptance in elementary school children, finding, too, that kids really do place a great deal of importance on athletic ability. Children seen as athletic by classmates were better liked and less likely to feel lonely, while unathletic kids often experienced sadness, isolation, and peer rejection.

What we find most disturbing, however, about this sad bit of human sociology are Thompson and Kindlon's observations that these boy-on-boy cruelties are *played out largely with adult sanction.* When classroom teachers and phys ed teachers and resource room aids make excuses for the teasing and choose to look the other way (e.g., ". . . boys being boys," ". . . part of being a kid"), dismiss it as inconsequential, or blame the victim for inducing it, targeted children are pretty much left to work their way free without the support of the adults hired to guide and protect them.

To be fair, however, a boy's distress is not always so obvious. In his book *Real Boys: Rescuing Our Sons from the Myths of Boyhood,* William Pollack coins the term *Boy Code,* referring to the hand-me-down set of social rules for males dictating that boys

> "To guarantee popularity in the average American high school, a guy must be able to claim either one of two assets: good looks or athletic prowess. Taken separately, only success in athletics can secure total acceptance, since physical appearance scores points only with the female constituency of the student body. Being a star athlete in high school is the quickest, most surefire way to ensure respect and admiration from all students."
>
> John Nikkah, *Our Boys Speak: Adolescent Boys Write About Their Inner Lives*

be tough and invincible. Pollack considers Boy Code to be partly to blame for the perpetuation of the "culture of adolescent cruelty" that preys on nonconformist boys. "The problem for those of us who want to help," says Pollack, "is that, on the outside, the boy who is having problems may seem cheerful and resilient while keeping inside the feelings that don't fit the male model— being troubled, lonely, afraid, desperate. Boys learn to wear the mask so skillfully . . . that it can be difficult to detect what is really going on when they are suffering at school, when their friendships are not working out, when they are being bullied, becoming depressed . . ."

The fact that social ordering among children is a natural and largely unpreventable occurrence is not a reason for us to look the other way when we see it happening. Nor should we become complacent when Boy Code mutes the collective voice of boys who need help but don't feel they can ask for it. "Being bullied is not just an unpleasant rite of passage through childhood," says Duane Alexander, M.D., director of the National Institute of Child Health and Human Development. He adds, "It's a public health problem that merits attention." Unfortunately, the impact of bullying doesn't necessarily get left behind with childhood. According to Alexander, "People who were bullied as children are more likely to suffer from depression and low self-esteem, well into adulthood, and the bullies themselves are more likely to engage in criminal behavior later in life."[3]

Even those adults who are actively on the lookout for bullying behaviors miss a lot of what goes on between kids. It's a smirk at the bus stop, a furtive exchange of glances during music class, a punch into the lower back while lining up to go to the cafeteria. Alan, the optometrist mentioned earlier, recalled some of his harassed, nonathletic friends fighting back in equally covert ways. "They became *intellectual* bullies," he described, lending support to the mythic schism between intelligence and athleticism. "Some jerk would throw an insult their way and invariably these guys would come right back with a very witty remark that would crack everyone up, leaving the first guy standing there with nothing to say. That was *my* kind of hero growing up."

Things do seem to get a little easier for boys like Alan once they get out of elementary and middle school. By high school, most boys have become more accepting of people's differences, and learned to appreciate accomplishments made off the playing field. A larger array of after-school clubs becomes available as well, offering not only a broader range of activities but along with that the opportunity to find like-minded peers. With remarkable prescience, Drew, a small-statured man who grew up to become a veterinarian, used his belief in a better future, one without teasing, as a way to endure a painful childhood. "I couldn't wait to grow up," he said to me after I mentioned that I was writing a book about boys who weren't into sports. "I never felt comfortable around boys who were very active and competitive. I didn't fit in with them and had trouble finding other boys who were like me. So I just kept telling myself that it would be better when I got older. And it did, in high school. But until then, it felt like it was taking forever."

THE SIGNS OF NONATHLETIC BOYS IN TROUBLE

- May complain of bellyaches, headaches, or general "I don't feel well" on gym days

- Hanging along the sidelines of physical activities or looking uncomfortable in unstructured social situations among boys (waiting for assembly, outside during a fire drill, walking from classroom to the school library)

- Boys who stay close to adults during play times or other free, unstructured times

- Going to the bathroom frequently before gym class or recess

WHAT TO DO:

- Parents can encourage their child's school to provide game activities for kids who don't like high-exertion activities but who also don't want to get stuck with only the swings as an alternative. Games like knock hockey, air hockey, and foosball offer great alternatives and safe havens for boys who are looking for noncontact, interactive activities or who simply need to be doing something. An industrious parent-teacher association can find second-hand tables through its own parent network, Craigslist, or yard sales.

- In place of traditional gym activities that favor the naturally athletic boys, schools could adopt short-session modules in which parent or teacher volunteers run pro-grams on introductory fencing, raft making, or boomer-ang throwing—novel activities that draw on a variety of skill sets.

- Schools can also be encouraged to identify boys a grade or two older who could be responsible for making sure everyone has something to do during recess and other unstructured times (lunch, waiting to be dismissed to the buses). These boys would be the same kinds of kids who are invited to be hallway guards, guides for new students, and the like. With kids so very anxious these days about being left by themselves and thus identified as "losers," knowing that there's a safe, older student to even stand around with if necessary provides some measure of relief.

Parents' Conundrum

Stand on the sidelines of any of the Saturday-morning Little League baseball games or YMCA soccer matches and you'll see at least a couple of boys looking as if they wished they were any-where but there. If they had it their way, they would be. They wouldn't be leaning up against a metal fence in a dugout or standing in the middle of a grassy field, learning the rules of a game they have little to no interest in playing. They are there only because their mom or dad thought they should be there.

"My dad made me play baseball because he loved it and he thought it would be a good sport for me," recalled forty-four-year-old Simon, who hasn't touched a bat or glove in thirty years. "I was a little short for my age but I was fast, so every January my dad took me over to the school to sign me up for spring baseball. But what I really loved was running and hiking—anything where my legs could carry me to new places. Plus, I was terrified of the ball. I'd play outfield and spend the whole time praying it wouldn't come my way. I spent nearly half my Little League career with my stomach lodged somewhere up in my throat. Thanks, Dad—that was a lot of fun."

Simon's father meant well, and probably would have been stunned to hear his son recount his baseball experience in this way. But parents' own enthusiasm for athletics, or insistence on a sports-team experience, sometimes flies in the face of their child's nature. In addition, the lines are often too fine to make easy distinctions between activities that are being encouraged and those that are being imposed.

Not all fathers' efforts to help their sons gain some sport experience turn out as poorly as they did for Simon. There are also good reasons *not* to give up on sports with boys who aren't naturally athletic. For one, being unathletic doesn't mean a boy won't enjoy playing a sport. He just may not be very good at it, or he may have to work harder at it than other boys in order to become reasonably competent, neither of which is reason to abandon the idea. And second, acquiring feelings of mastery over one's body, in terms of being able to make it do what you want it to do, is an important developmental task for all kids—boys or girls, athletic or not. Our bodies are with us for life, and a child's pride in being able to control it—even if it isn't the stuff of sports legends—will go far in encouraging him or her to take care of it, with physical exercise or activity being an important part of that.

Simon's experience with baseball highlights an issue that often poses a big dilemma for parents: When does pushing a boy into an activity he doesn't like—because it's believed he *will* like it or *should learn* to like it—become an affront to his genuine self? And what's the thing to do if getting the boy to the activity becomes a regular battle between a parent and child? What if there are more and more tears or tantrums or angry exchanges? If the parents relent, will it be setting a precedent for future challenges their son will face? Are they enabling him if they allow him to avoid sports, or are they respecting his individuality? Doesn't he need sports to get into college? To have friends? To feel good about himself?

"I was trying to get him interested in tennis," said Brad, talking about his fourteen-year-old son, Noah. "We have so little in common as it is, with him not liking most sports. This was supposed to be a good thing—him and me, Sunday mornings, you know? But we'd just end up arguing about going all the time. Finally I said, 'This is crazy! I'm doing this to get closer to my son and all it's doing is making us fight!'"

Back to Drew, the guy who waited forever to feel at home socially. He was fortunate to be brought up in a family whose values matched his own personality pretty well. "My parents were not real into it [sports] or not into it," he recalled. "They were very passive individuals, not 'go-getters.' Most of their success, whether it was their business or being recognized in their community, came about pretty organically. It was easy for us not to chase something that didn't draw us in naturally."

PROCESSING SPORTS EXPERIENCES TOGETHER WITH YOUR NONATHLETIC SON . . .

If your son does not naturally gravitate toward sports and you're encouraging him to get more involved in them, try to keep a dialogue going on between the two of you about his experiences—and yours, too. It's especially important to do this if there is any question about your son's enjoyment of or comfort with sports, or any question about to whom it matters more that he play—you or him.

GIVE HIM OPPORTUNITIES TO SAY:

"I really don't want to play this but I feel like if I don't you'll be mad at me . . ."

GIVE YOURSELF OPPORTUNITIES TO SAY:

"I've worried about that, and don't want you to feel as if you have to do a certain activity in order to win my approval. I just want you to feel that you can join a game of basketball or baseball so that you don't always wind up on the outside looking in. *I* don't care that you prefer other things to sports, but other people do, and I think it would be good for you to know how to hang in a game if you ever felt you wanted to—or felt you needed to . . ."

I think of boys like Drew as having been very lucky. These were boys who were able to look up at their parents and find radiant eyes that told them, *You are ours and we are blessed to have you and we want to know who you are.* Boys who aren't as lucky experience a self-worth that is more conditional; they are good only as long as they fit what the other party wants or needs them to be.

Helping Boys to Cope

Years ago I went to hear a lecture about children who struggle with long-standing learning difficulties in school. A question from an audience member about enhancing self-esteem in these kids led the speaker to make a distinction between the "feel-good" that kids get from hearing their parents praise them for their accomplishments and the feel-good they get when they realize their parents really respect them, the sort of thing they might learn by overhearing their mom or dad singing their praises to another adult.

This is a critical distinction in a subject (esteem building) that continues to generate questions even after decades of study and an extraordinary amount of attention. Kids whose parents are trying hard to shore up their self-esteem will often hear that they did a good job on such and such test or project, or a wonderful job watching their younger brother. This is terrific feedback; it allows a child to feel good about something he or she did. However, when children overhear a parent bragging about them to a third party, they hear something very different. They hear, *I'm so proud of my kid and I'm telling you about him not in order to make him feel better, but because thinking about what he does makes me feel better.* So for an eight-year-old kid who fears that his poor hand-eye coordination and lack of interest in sports has been a big disappointment to his father, overhearing his dad boasting about him to another adult is, well, a big deal. He realizes, *Wow, my dad thinks I'm the bomb . . . even though I can't catch a Frisbee. And he must really mean it, because he wasn't expecting me to hear any of this.*

It gets even better for a child when he learns that his parent's pride in him stems not just from *something he did* but from *who he is.* How perfect is that for the kid who will never be the fastest, strongest, biggest, or best, yet who exhibits immeasurably worthy qualities such as kindness, compassion, or patience. By isolating, recognizing, and then rewarding these traits, publicly as well as privately, we can begin to level the playing fields for kids on which, historically, might has determined right.

Unavoidably, all children endure a mixed assortment of bad experiences over the years having to do in one way or another with being excluded, feeling left out, or getting bullied. But these bad experiences don't always have to become bad memories. Bad experiences can be disempowered when there are people in kids' lives who say, *No, this is wrong,* or, *What happened to you is lousy but it is not personal.* Bad experiences are disempowered when caring adults are able to correctly identify the children who are thinking, *There must be something very wrong with me that I'm the butt of so many jokes,* and then help them digest what has taken place within a broader social and cultural context.

There are abundant opportunities for parents, teachers, relatives, coaches, and other youth mentors to neutralize the negative messages that nonconforming kids pick up from their environs, but it's not always easy for everyone to take advantage of them. By the time you recognize an opportunity, it's already passed or you're stumped trying to come up with the right thing to say. Plus, intervening on the fly like that can be intimidating. People become anxious about saying the wrong thing and find all kinds of reasons to pass on the moment and wait until the "next" time, when they think they'll be better prepared. But sometimes that next time never comes, and besides, all the eloquent phrasing you think you're going to have ready that next time won't compare to the clumsy collection of mismatched but beautiful words telling a boy it mattered more to his mom or dad or teacher or uncle to come out with something that would help him feel better than to sound halfway decent saying it.

In addition to helping kids digest these experiences constructively, parents, as well as other supervising adults including teachers, hall monitors, bus drivers, cafeteria workers, coaches, librarians, and janitorial staff, can become aware of the times and places that nonathletic boys in a community or particular school are likely to get ambushed—locker rooms in the gym, isolated corners of the playground, the rear seats on school buses, the unsupervised area right outside doorways where kids gather and wait—and provide more coverage. Parents can also help their sons plan ahead for loosely structured situations in which they are more likely to get self-conscious than teased—being lined up by height, when sports teams are being chosen for gym, during the annual Presidential Physical Fitness Challenge.

Spotting troublesome scenes and calling the instigators out in that moment are very effective deterrents to aggressive behavior among kids—*as long as no one is ever humiliated or unduly embarrassed in the process.* Nobody ever rises to a higher standard of any sort by being made to feel bad about him or herself. Besides, it's unkind, and erodes the trust between adults and kids. There really aren't any scripts for this, but the objective is to induce just enough self-consciousness or discomfort for the instigator to want to get out of the spotlight, which he can best do by stopping the offensive behavior.

Here's an example. Let's say you're walking alongside a bunch of children who are returning to their classroom following a trip to the school library. Kevin is making fun of Tyler because Tyler has taken out some books—five of them, to be exact. "Whoa, that looks like a lot of fun, Tyler," he says facetiously in front of his buddies, who comply with the expected laughter. "I wish I could read all weekend, too!" More laughter. So you go over and say, quietly and not angrily, "You make fun of people for reading?" and wait, as if you're seriously expecting him to answer, which he won't. Kevin won't like that his "joking around"—which is how he'd defend it if he had the chance—has been identified for what it really is—flagrant teasing, and because of that, he'll be much less likely to try to return to it. In contrast, being told to "settle down" or "stop talking in the hallways" doesn't even get kids' attention for more than the time it takes for the teacher to turn away. Then they start right back up again. In the first example, it's as if the teacher is saying, *Look, I don't want to make a big deal out of this but I also don't want to pretend that it was "just joking around." It was mean. It wasn't funny. Make it stop.*

Here's another example. A lunch mom decides to go eyeball to eyeball with the ringleader of a crew of three fourth graders who have made it their job to provide live commentary on the lunchtime choices of certain, less popular boys. "What could possibly feel good about making fun of people for what they eat?" she can say to him, within earshot of his young cronies. Then, knowing it will never come, she waits for his answer, implying that it is not a rhetorical question, but rather one to be taken seriously. It will register with the boy on some level, and if he's lucky, someone else will make a similar comment in a similar situation, pressing his conscience into service so that it eventually becomes more taxing for him to indulge his ruthless amusements than to abandon them altogether.

Or, in another example, a father picking up his kids notices a group of brash, rowdy boys in the schoolyard, bragging about how fast they are, and calls out to them, congenially, "You guys talk like being fast is the most important thing in this world!" He doesn't need to say anything else, or wait around for a response. By now both disarmed and self-conscious, these brash boys will most likely just stop talking. But they heard what the dad had to say about bragging rights to being fast, even if they don't agree. In addition, for any boy with questionable physical agility or speed who happened to be in the vicinity, this father's remark would serve as a nice public vote of support, and the fact that it was totally uncontrived and spoken independently of his presence makes it even better.

Similarly, a mom hearing her son chide a younger brother about his poor performance in their summer camp's annual relay race can walk over to him and pointedly ask, "Of all the things you could say to him at a time like this, why on earth would you pick that?" The mother's oblique reference to her son's sadly lacking empathic sensibilities is a more elegant and effective way of prompting sensitivity in the boy than the conventional lecture about "being nice."

And what about the boy whose feelings are hurt? What should we be saying to him? Anything that will help him feel less alone and less like some freak, things referring to . . .

. . . how people in our culture expect all boys to play sports and that it's terribly unfair to the many who don't

. . . what he can do or say whenever he is getting teased for not playing sports or being good at physical games

. . . whether he has anyone at home or at school who knows that he sometimes feels left out because of not wanting to get involved in sports or other kinds of intense physical activity

. . . whether he has anyone in his life who is helping him to discover the things he is or can become good at

. . . whether he has an adult to count on who will stop any mistreatment by peers or siblings

. . . how trying hard to fit in sometimes makes things worse

. . . how sometimes, when you are seen as different, it is better just to own the difference than to pretend that you are something you're not

These conversations usually take place in the sanctity and privacy of therapists' rooms and school counselors' offices, but we'd like to see them taking place elsewhere, too—in living rooms and in cars, in classrooms and auditoriums, in school superintendents' offices, on playgrounds and in parks, in the boardrooms of synagogues and churches and township recreation leagues. Classical therapy can be terrifically helpful to children needing to recover their self-esteem, confidence, or dignity, but it is often isolated from the rest of the child's life and almost always called into service only after damage has been done.

Our vision of helping these kids includes therapy but other interventions, too: education, advocacy, dialogue, and community engagement around the issues of playground politics, gender expectations, and the importance in our culture of sports, winning, and being the "best." This is what can prompt a larger kind of change, i.e., change *within the consciousness of our communities themselves,* and their human architects. Nothing short of that will show these boys just how valued they are in a society that still measures many of its heroes by standards few people can ever really meet.

. . .

Parents are the major artisans in shaping the way their children think about gender and gender roles. They serve as models for the kinds of attitudes their children will develop toward themselves and toward other people, and they are also the filters through which their sons and daughters will hear society's messages about what it means to be a boy and what it means to be a girl. Some nonathletic, noncompetitive, introverted boys will grow up knowing unequivocally that they are valued and cherished members of their family, and that what they mean to everyone has nothing to do with how fast they run or how many times they scored in the game. Others hear a different message, even though it was never intended.

"I always knew that my dad loved me and all that," thirty-two-year-old Aaron said. "I never doubted it for a moment. But the thing was that there were all these times when my dad would come home from work really excited, and charge through the front door calling for my brother to come out and practice shooting some basketball, and I'd think, 'God, he never calls out for me like that.'" It was difficult for Aaron to recite these memories out loud. He loved his father and knew that his father adored him. Speaking this way made him feel as if he was betraying his dad, and yet Aaron's inability to draw from his father that degree of enthusiasm had stayed with him all these years. "As a kid, I really admired my brother and looked up to him, which made the whole thing worse because I'd get really angry at him for being able to get my dad so excited. I knew it wasn't his fault, but I kept wishing that one of those times he'd just stop our dad and say, 'Hey, Dad, what about Aaron?! He's an awesome kid, don't you think? Plays a mean game of Scrabble, and no one can ever beat him at Twister either.'"

Truthfully, many parents do have a different relationship with their athletic sons than they do with their sons who aren't into sports. They love all their children the same, they'll always say—and mean it. It's just that they—and especially fathers—are more "at home" with a boy who meets gender expectations. They feel as if they have a better idea of what to do with him and how to raise him. Parenting is hard enough when you do have a vision of the role you are going to play: Dads play catch or work on cars with their sons, and moms go shopping with their daughters, an admittedly reductionist script for family relations. And lots of moms and dads actually do those things even though they don't enjoy them; their value is in the template they provide for the relationships they are trying to have with their children. But when the template doesn't fit the child, many parents don't know where to turn. Some use the template anyway and make everyone miserable. Some just turn away. But there is a third option—creating a new template.

CHAPTER TWO

What Kind of Boy Doesn't Like to Play Sports?

It's hard for some people to imagine that sports and physical games don't appeal to all boys—at least not without there being a "problem" of some kind. But with all the different combinations of temperament, personality, physique, and neurophysiology that are spun and then filtered through one-of-a-kind collections of life experiences, strict gender homogeneity is probably one of the last things we should be expecting.

A more reliable rule of thumb may be this: Generally speaking, if you're good at something, you'll want to do more of it, and if you're not good at something, you'll want either to work at it until you are good, or move on to something that's a more natural fit. That said, sometimes people are good at certain activities but still want no part of them and that's their prerogative; I don't believe anyone should feel beholden to advancing a talent of theirs they don't enjoy expressing, no matter how good it is or how much others enjoy it. Being really good at something shouldn't mean you then *have* to do it.

Doing well and taking pleasure in playing sports or other types of physical games depends upon at least a few things in a child's life lining up correctly. For one, they need a body that can run and catch and climb reasonably well, and doing those things has to feel good enough to the kid to want to do them again and again. They also need opportunities and time to exercise their physical skills, which is less a given than some might realize. Some young kids simply aren't allowed outside after school because there is no adult at home to supervise or because the neighborhood is unsafe. Some are allowed outside but don't go, finding the television or computer screen more compelling. Children who grow up on properties such as livestock or produce farms, or other kinds of family-run businesses, are often needed to work before and/or after school. They might be physically fit but never have played an organized sport. That all children grow up playing is deceptively idyllic and only a partial truth.

> "Our kids now watch *Survivor* on TV as entertainment instead of playing Swiss Family Robinson out back."
>
> Beth

Some boys don't *dislike* sports so much as simply prefer other activities. *Last Child in the Woods* author, Richard Louv, writes about boys who love unstructured fantasy play, the kind of play that takes place outdoors, not in man-made parks but in ungroomed wooded areas with ravines, rocky inclines, and patches of natural vegetation. Here, away from the sports-heavy agenda of schools and neighborhood yards, good play rests not on physical strength and agility but on a different, versatile set of faculties such as imagination and language skills and ingenuity, flipping—if only for a few hours—the conventional social ordering of boys on its head.

Other boys like the physical nature of traditional boy play but aren't cut out for the discipline or regimentation of team sports. They chafe at the need to comply with coaches and other officials, or get restless with the stop-and-go rhythm of practice or play. These boys may instead gravitate toward sports where they have more control over the game itself, such as racquetball or table tennis, or opt for more solitary activities such as hiking or biking, where their need for independence enhances rather than interferes with the experience. Some boys just don't like competing at all or like it only in nonphysical, nonsporting arenas, such as chess or music. Or, maybe they love competing and are really good at their game, but have chosen sports and activities more commonly selected by girls, such as horseback riding or dance or gymnastics.

There are also lots of boys who get seriously injured playing sports and don't want to play anymore, or don't recover psychologically at the rate at which everyone thinks they should. But when it's your face that collided with a high-velocity ball, only you will really be able to tell when you're ready to return to the field. For some kids that never happens, and for those kids, all the prompting by restless coaches and eager parents and friends won't make their overwhelming anxiety about getting hit again go away. You can't promise them that it won't happen again, because it can. They know it, and feel patronized when you insist otherwise. Even noting the very low probability of such an injury happening again won't make it any easier for the child to get back on the field; half of a one percent chance is still a chance, and that's enough to feed anxiety for a long time. Ever implored to "be more rational," to "man up," to "toughen up," or to "get the hell back in there," these unfortunate boys (and girls) face a dilemma with the wretched choice of either disappointing the grown-ups or playing with their hearts in their throats.

But what are we teaching him if we let him quit just because he's afraid of the ball? parents will ask. Here's what you're teaching him: You're teaching him to speak up about decisions that affect his well-being. You're teaching him that you will listen closely to what he says. You are teaching him that, in your eyes, he is a credible figure. You are teaching him that he doesn't have to disguise his real feelings in order to sustain your approval. You are teaching him that people may not always like how their mind responds to an unexpected event, but it's a reminder that we can't control everything about ourselves. You are teaching him that you will never put your need for him to be a certain kind of athlete or boy or person ahead of his need to feel safe. He's afraid of the ball. If he wants to work through it, help him do that with the aid of time, patience, an appreciation of his reticence to jump back into play, an understanding coach, and maybe a sport psychologist. But if he doesn't, consider that he might be one of those kids who have trouble locating objects in space, assessing their rate of movement or trajectory, and then transmitting the information to their hand in time to make the catch. Or consider that he might be better able to demonstrate perseverance in another sport or activity. If *he* doesn't care about moving on to something different, why should anyone else?

Introverts, Extroverts, and Traditional Masculine Ideals

It's easy to imagine boys who are lively and extroverted indulging a love of physical, interactive games, but what about more introverted boys? Reflective, circumspect, and partial to solitary or small-group play, these boys, according to Marti Olsen Laney, author of *The Hidden Gifts of the Introverted Child: Helping Your Child Thrive in an Extroverted World*, have social and recreational needs that are very different from the ones their more extroverted peers enjoy. Whereas extroverts seek lots of stimulation—the kind you get from sports, for instance—introverted children generally are more comfortable in the internal world of impressions, ideas, and feelings. Many of these boys also have strong needs for privacy; in fact, the same type of interacting that energizes the extroverted kid actually drains the introvert. It's easy to see how being with a lot of people for long periods of time, characteristic of many sports-related activities, can be very taxing for this type of child.

However we are, if nothing else, a nation of extroverts living in a culture seeped in overstimulation. Americans like doing things and going places, and they like doing those things with other people. Most would wonder why anyone would choose to live differently. Laney points out the inherent devaluation of introversion within our cultural mores, which support people who are putting themselves out there, speaking up, winning contests (real or imagined), and achieving in very visible ways. She notes, too, that interacting with introverts can actually be unsettling for extroverts. To the extroverted individual, who is accustomed to interacting very quickly, directly, and outwardly with others, an introverted person, who processes things internally—and therefore privately—can appear mysterious or unassertive or even a little aloof. These factors, in addition to our culture's emphasis on socializing and group acceptance, create problems for children who simply prefer different settings for learning or playing, or who aren't as concerned about how they fit in with the larger crowd as their parents or relatives or teachers might think they should be. For these reasons, both Laney and Isabel Myers, author of *Gifts Differing: Understanding Personality Type,* stress the need for parents and educators to talk about introversion and extroversion as different temperament styles and not as gauges for what is or isn't healthy socialization. As Laurie Helgoe noted in her article on introverts in *Psychology Today,* "Their biggest challenge is not to feel like outsiders in their own culture."[1]

Just in case anyone thought that with a little push over the hump, introverted kids could become more like their extroverted peers—who outnumber them three to one by the way—consider Laney's caveat that pressure to function outside their comfort zones only makes introverts anxious and uncomfortable. And shouldn't it? If they were ever to have thrived as extroverts, they would have done so long ago. It's not their preferred or most functional way of living; being imposed upon like that is just one more way introverted boys are told, *Yeah, you're fine, kid, but if you could just be a little more like . . . you know . . . those guys/so-and-so/ your brother . . . well, I think you might have a lot more friends/be more popular/feel happier* . . . When teacher and researcher Bonnie Golden studied junior college students to investigate whether extroverts had higher self-esteem than introverts because they better fit cultural norms, she found that her sample of extroverts did.[2] The central condition raising self-esteem for extroverted subjects? *Accomplishing goals.* The central condition for the introverts in the study? *Being appreciated.* If what we're after is a well-adjusted boy who likes himself and exhibits the confidence to pursue his own genuine areas of interest, then what he needs isn't a nudge toward what "other boys do" but a nod from the adults in his life who recognize what it takes to own your person and live your life accordingly.

Learning and Developmental Disabilities Affecting Children's Physical Skills

Learning disabilities are disorders that affect a person's ability to acquire, organize, retain, understand, or use verbal or nonverbal information. They are due to impairments in one or more of the psychological processes underlying perception, cognition, memory, or learning—faculties such as processing the speed at which an object is moving, or making inferences. Developmental disabilities appear in infancy or childhood and interfere with the normal development of language, motor, or cognitive skills; cerebral palsy and autism are examples. Language-based learning disabilities are specific disabilities affecting reading, spelling, writing, or math computation. Usually, they do not affect a person's physical abilities, and in fact, there have been many successful and even elite athletes with documented learning disabilities: basketball Hall of Famer Magic Johnson, Olympic decathlon gold medalist Bruce Jenner, Olympic diving gold medalist Greg Louganis, and boxing icon and Olympic gold medalist Muhammad Ali, to name a few.

Non-language-based learning disabilities, however, often do affect a person's physical abilities. These are the nonverbal learning disabilities, and they compromise a person's executive functions, meaning his or her ability to plan, assign priorities, regulate emotions, solve problems, control their impulses, and set goals.

In addition, individuals, and especially children, with this kind of disability have trouble picking up on *nonverbal* information—facial expressions, body language, and the like. They may laugh at something that wasn't supposed to be funny, or not laugh when everyone else in the class does. These kinds of misinterpretations reflect their difficulties with social perception, and subsequently, with perspective taking and social interaction at large.

Learning disabilities frequently go undetected in a child's early years, coming to the attention of teachers or parents only when they try to master the more complex types of learning and motor skills that come with grades four and five. By that time, such boys (and girls) have already spent years frustrated by their inability to run or throw as well as their peers, not understanding that it had nothing to do with how hard they tried but rather with the particular way in which their brain communicates with their body.

So is it possible that some of the boys who don't like to play sports have learning disabilities? In a word, yes. It's estimated that 8 to 10 percent of American children under the age of eighteen have some type of learning disability. Boys diagnosed with learning disabilities outnumber girls by about three to one, but whether this higher prevalence is due to a biological vulnerability or to referral bias (meaning, boys with academic problems are being referred for special education at a higher rate than girls because of other problematic behaviors, such as hyperactivity) isn't certain.

Although learning and developmental disabilities are both lifelong conditions, interventions such as special education, speech and language therapy, occupational and reading therapies, psychoeducational therapy, and medication help children reduce the impact of skill deficits and manage some of the symptoms. Some children are diagnosed with several overlapping disabilities, while others are found to have only one isolated cognitive or motor skill problem for which they are able to compensate over time and with little impact on their lives.

Let's look at how certain disabilities can affect a child's ability to engage successfully in sports and other physical play activities:

Motor Skills Deficits

Dyspraxia is a learning disability that affects a person's ability to plan out and sequence motor activities (movement). With this condition, the brain has difficulty conceiving, organizing, and carrying out sequences of behaviors that are new or unpracticed. Therefore, dyspraxic children often have problems learning physical skills in the first place, as well as then building on top of these simpler motor skills to master more complex ones (e.g., learning to throw balls after having learned to catch them). They will exhibit difficulties with fine and/or gross motor control, balance, and direction, and be noticed having trouble climbing stairs, using playground equipment, or riding a bike.

Weaknesses in comprehension and information processing can exacerbate the problems experienced by people with dyspraxia, resulting in low self-esteem and other emotional and behavioral troubles. In some children, dyspraxia will present as part of a more comprehensive developmental disorder known as sensory integration dysfunction. This disorder causes problems in a person's ability to accurately process information received through the senses, creating abnormal degrees of oversensitivity or under-sensitivity to touch, light, and/or sound. Sensory integration dys-function, and its impact on a child's physical skills, is explained in greater detail below.

Developmental coordination disorder is one of the developmental disabilities affecting motor activity. Similar to dyspraxia, it is marked primarily by poor coordination. Kids with this disorder trip over their own feet, run into other children, have trouble holding objects, or show unsteady gaits but otherwise often develop normally. Poor eye-hand coordination keeps a lot of them from catching balls well, as does, in some, their poor control over eye muscles. Dyspraxia and developmental coordination disorder are distinct disorders, although the two may appear together in the same child; they affect an estimated 2 to 10 percent of the population in varying degrees.[3] In fact, poor performance in sports is listed as one of several possible criteria for developmental coordination disorder in the *Diagnostic and Statistical Manual of Mental Disorders, Fourth Edition,* the mental health bible of psychiatric diagnoses.

With specialized attention and teaching techniques, it is possible for many children with developmental motor deficits to improve their motor skills over time. However, while research indicates that these skills can be improved to a significant extent, in most cases they will never truly match those of the child's peers.

WHAT MOTOR DEFICITS MEAN FOR PLAYING SPORTS:

- The child's gait may be awkward, impacting speed and agility; he may be the kid who's always tagged "it."

- He may have trouble learning to ride a scooter or bike.

- He may have trouble catching and holding balls, or throwing objects based on what his eyes are seeing.

- He may have trouble passing a ball or other object to another person.

- He may be easily knocked off balance or knocked over.

- He may not recover quickly enough from stumbling to prevent a fall.

Visual-Motor Deficits

Visual-motor integration is what we commonly think of as eye-body or eye-hand coordination. It is where the eyes tell the muscles what to do and how to do it. Whereas the problems in fine and gross motor coordination listed under "motor skills deficits" are the result of problems in the motor system itself, visual-motor deficits are caused by problems in how the information taken in by the eyes is processed and communicated to the muscles. Problems with gross motor eye-body coordination will lead to difficulties with "big muscle" activities such as bike riding, while fine motor eye-hand coordination problems will affect "smaller muscle" movements, making it hard for kids to write neatly or work through assignments quickly.

Visual Processing Deficits

Visual processing refers to the ability to *make sense* of information taken in through the eyes. It has nothing to do with one's sight or sharpness of vision. Difficulties with visual processing affect how visual information is *interpreted* or *processed*. Therefore, a person with visual processing problems may have 20/20 vision, but have difficulties discriminating foreground from background, or determining the position of objects in space. The eyes *look*, but the brain *sees*.[4]

WHAT VISUAL-MOTOR DEFICITS MEAN FOR PLAYING SPORTS:

- The child may have problems with activities that involve steering (riding bicycles or scooters, maneuvering amusement-park bumper cars) and aiming (throwing objects to other people, catching them, playing darts, archery).

- Playground games such as jacks and jumping rope could be especially challenging, as could table games like billiards and foosball (table soccer).

Visual processing deficits can interfere with a person's ability to connect sights with sound, making it hard for that person to know where to look when trying to locate the sound's source. Problems connecting sight with touch mean a person may not be able to determine how much pressure is needed to move or lift an object by just looking at it. If the problem is connecting sight with movement sensations, a person's spatial awareness will be impaired, affecting the ability to move fluidly around obstacles or furniture.

WHAT VISUAL PROCESSING DEFICITS MEAN FOR PLAYING SPORTS:

- The child could have difficulties throwing a basketball into the hoop, or hitting a ball with the bat.

- Games like Ping-Pong, where players must quickly discern figure-ground relationships, may also be difficult.

- He might have trouble grabbing the flag off another player in flag football.

- He might have trouble orienting to an instructor or coach yelling directions from the sidelines.

- He might have problems holding on to a ball that he just caught.

Visual-Spatial and Motor-Spatial Deficits

Visual-spatial performance refers to using sight to discriminate differences or determine the relative location of one object to another. Children with visual-spatial deficits may have difficulty making visual images in order to "see something in the mind's eye" or "get the picture." They may also have difficulty differentiating left from right, or remembering visual images.

Problems with spatial-relations skills show up not only in people's visual processing but in their motor processing as well. Whereas visual-spatial performance refers to using sight to discriminate differences, motor-spatial performance refers to making the body move accurately and smoothly in relation to objects in space. Of course, many activities demand some combination of visual-spatial and motor-spatial skill. Visual spatial processing problems appear frequently in children diagnosed with nonverbal learning disabilities.

Here's a good illustration of the difference between visual-spatial and motor-spatial skills, and how it shows up in some children. In a Web article entitled "Spatial Relations and Learning," authors Carol Stockdale and Carol Possin contrasted three fourteen-year-old basketball players who were learning to shoot free throws. The first boy, with no discernible deficits, became an average free-throw shooter after a reasonable amount of practice under a coach's supervision. The second boy had weak visual-spatial skills, but strong motor-spatial skills. Therefore, even though he had excellent control over his muscles, he was unable to judge the distance to the basket with his eye and direct the ball. He learned to shoot free throws with relative accuracy by learning to "feel" how much push his muscles had to supply to hit the hoop. The third boy had the reverse: weak motor-spatial skills but strong visual-spatial skills. As a child, he'd been described as "clumsy" and had to work hard to master even the most basic of motor skills. He did, however, have excellent visual control, meaning that he could watch his pencil intently and "force" it to go where he wanted it to go, compensating for his poor motor control. This boy surprised everyone by going out for junior high basketball and surprised them again when he showed himself to be an accurate shooter. Depending upon his visual control to guide his shot, this third boy seemed almost to will the ball through the hoop with his eyes.

The authors shared another illuminative story about how undetected learning disabilities can impact sport performance in a major way: A soccer coach was puzzled over the erratic play of one of his players, who, as a forward, played poorly. The boy was now asking to play goalie, and the coach wasn't too sure that this was a good idea. "He did the craziest things," this coach was saying to another coach. "In one game he dribbled right out-of-bounds three times . . . Never took his eye off the ball. Just forgot where he was. Looked surprised as anything when the ref whistled."

The coach went on to describe the boy as very coordinated, *but for only one thing at a time.* According to the boy himself, he could dribble *or* he could keep track of the other players *or* he could monitor his position on the field. Interestingly, when the boy finally convinced the coach to give him a shot at playing goalie, he proved to be excellent.

Stockdale and Possin explained the variable quality of this boy's play by pointing out that while his coordination and balance were excellent, his ability to monitor his position and keep track of his location on the field while moving was poor. However, when playing from a relatively fixed position, i.e., that of a goalie, he was able to track the ball. If he had had to move with the ball down the field, he would have run into problems again. Basically, this boy was able to do well in any activity in which he could track the ball from pretty much the same position each time. The authors speculated that he would make a good base-

WHAT SPATIAL DEFICITS MEAN FOR PLAYING SPORTS:

- The child may have trouble tracking moving objects, for example, knowing when to swing a tennis racket or baseball bat in relation to the approaching ball's movement through space.

- He may have difficulty staying within bounds.

- He may run the wrong way when a field is divided into different goal areas.

- He may have a lot of trouble with sports requiring an awareness of one's body position in space—wrestling, for example, as well as gymnastics and diving.

- He may have trouble throwing accurately to other players while they are moving on the field or court.

ball catcher as well, depending on how well he handled the unpredictable foul balls or wild pitches. Analyses like this make a person realize just how fine-tuned the neurophysiology of elite athletes must be.

Sensory Integration Dysfunction

First coined by occupational therapist Dr. A. Jean Ayers, the term *sensory integration dysfunction* refers to problems in the neurological process responsible for organizing sensation from within one's own body and from the external environment. It is what allows our bodies to adapt to and function in different environments.[5] A person can have sensory problems within the tactile system (touch), the proprioceptive system (body awareness), or the vestibular system (motion and balance).

Sensory problems within the tactile system
Tactile refers to our sense of touch. Kids with tactile sensitivity will make a big deal out of minor injuries or avoid messy play such as that in sand or mud. Sometimes they will develop what's called tactile defensiveness, where they react negatively to light touch or even the anticipation of touch. According to child psychiatrist Dr. Stanley Greenspan, author of *Playground Politics: Understanding the Emotional Life of Your School-Aged Child,* socialization problems are common among these kids because they have difficulty with the give-and-take, rough-and-tumble world of playground politics.

Sensory problems within the proprioceptive system

Proprioception is the unconscious awareness of one's body position. It tells us about the position of our body parts in relationship to each other and to the external environment. An example of an intact proprioceptive system would be the ability to pick up an egg with just the right amount of pressure and, without breaking it, place it on a plate.

Children with problems in this area show a poor awareness of their body position and may overshoot or undershoot specific movements. A lot of these kids also have trouble holding their posture, which in turn affects their balance and sequencing of movements, giving the impression of being "klutzy."

Sensory problems within the vestibular system

The vestibular system is the system located in the inner ear that tells you where your head and body are in relation to the earth. Its primary function is to register the movements of the eyes, head, and neck and respond to the pull of gravity, and then send this information to the nervous system. You use your vestibular system to determine whether you are moving or standing still, and whether the objects around you are moving or stationary.

Kids with vestibular dysfunction may have difficulty processing information about gravity, balance, and movement through space. The ones who have **hypersensitive** systems have a low tolerance for movements such as swinging, spinning, and sliding, and are likely to be cautious and slow moving when they play.

They are often afraid of falling, even when no real danger of falling exists. Hypersensitive children become motion sick rather easily, making riding in cars, elevators, and escalators uncomfortable, if not a little dicey.

The kids who have **hyposensitive** systems have an increased tolerance for movement. They may like seesaws and trampolines more than most children, and not be able to tell when they are dizzy or about to fall. They may also crave excessive movement such as bouncing on furniture, assuming upside-down positions, or rocking.

Other symptoms of vestibular dysfunction can include poor postural control (loose floppy body, often slumps or leans), poor motor planning (movement), and poor bilateral coordination (difficulty making both feet or hands work together).

Elaborating further, Carol Kranowitz, one of the leading clinicians in the area of sensory integration disorders and author of *The Out-of-Sync Child*, points out that there are three different categories of dysfunction within each of the systems noted above, listing them as follows: (a) disorders in *modulating* sensory information, (b) disorders in *discriminating* between different sensory information, and (c) disorders in *moving* based on sensory information.

Problems modulating sensory information cause people to overrespond, underrespond, or fluctuate in response to sensory input in a manner that is disproportional to that input. Some

WHAT SENSORY INTEGRATION DYSFUNCTION
MEANS FOR PLAYING SPORTS:

- Children with tactile dysfunction may avoid contact sports and activities where they are likely to get very sweaty or dirty.

- Children with proprioceptive dysfunction may have particular difficulty with activities requiring good body awareness and stability of posture. Many are prone to tripping or bumping into things, while others have trouble knowing how much muscular force to exert in a particular situation, resulting in complaints about playing "too rough."

- Children with vestibular dysfunction may exhibit exaggerated fears of falling, and so avoid any sports involving heights (gymnastics, horseback riding, diving). They may also not feel comfortable sitting in bleachers as a spectator. Hypersensitive kids may go to great lengths to avoid any playground equipment that involves swinging, sliding, or spinning.

common types of sensory modulation disorders include oversensitivity to touch or sound, and difficulty adjusting quickly to different environments. As an example of an intact system of modulation, Kranowitz gives the following: a kid who is able to cheer loudly for his favorite basketball team and then immediately shift gears to be able to stand in line to order refreshments.

An example of poor sensory modulation to the sense of touch would be a child who, when getting foam soap on her hand, withdraws it abruptly and shouts out as if in pain.

Problems discriminating between different sensory information make it hard for people to correctly register (recognize) the information they are getting from their body's senses. Therefore, they may have trouble knowing which way is up when they're upside down, or telling the difference between a penny and a nickel through feel. This can also make it hard for them to distinguish between a safe touch and a threatening touch. A brother who excitedly grabs his sister's arm in order to share some news might be surprised (and offended) to find that his sister thinks he just shoved her.

Problems moving based on sensory information interfere with a person's *ability to* conceive, organize, and carry out a sequence of new or unpracticed actions. This is the same dyspraxia that was described earlier in the chapter. Again, this type of disorder affects a person's ability to analyze his or her motor performance in order to make adjustments for improving the next attempt, accounting for a slow learning curve when it comes to physical activities.

What You Can Do to Help
Boys Whose Disabilities
Affect Their Physical Skills

All the different disabilities described above are listed under nice, tidy categories, but in reality, there is a lot of overlap. Discerning which disability or disabilities might be responsible for which symptoms is often a complex process of evaluation and observation. Martin Kutscher, who wrote *Kids in the Syndrome Mix of ADHD, LD, Asperger's, Tourette's, Bipolar, and More!: The One Stop Guide for Parents, Teachers, and Other Professionals,* points out that many children with developmental disorders or disabilities have multiple symptoms and issues, making it hard to distinguish between learning disabilities, attention deficit hyperactivity disorder, autistic spectrum disorders such as Asperger's syndrome, sensory integration disorders, depression, obsessive-compulsive disorders, Tourette's, and central processing disorders, among others. Muddying the clinical picture even more, not only can problems from one type of disorder imitate those from another, but many of the conditions are comorbid, meaning they exist in tandem with one or more of the others (an example of this is a child with Asperger's who also exhibits sensory integration dysfunction, obsessive-compulsive symptoms, and anxiety). Even with all this lack of clarity, there are ways for parents to attenuate some of the effects of their child's learning disabilities or other developmental disorders on his enjoyment and mastery of various sports and out-door activities.

Early intervention

One of the most important things you can do for a child who is showing signs of a learning disability is to *act on it* by consulting with the child's pediatrician, teachers, guidance counselor, and/or school psychologist. In cases of motor or sensory-motor dysfunction, where the window of opportunity for remediation is early and brief, acting on your suspicions is critical. Pass on the temptation to "wait and see," and don't be dissuaded by your child's demonstration of excellent skills in other areas. Without ever knowing it, many gifted children learn to compensate so well for their learning disabilities that the problems remain masked for years.

Help your child compensate for deficits in one area with strengths in another

Like the three basketball players learning to shoot free throws, kids can make up for weak visual-spatial skills with strong motor skills, and vice versa. If you know the specific functions affected by your son's disability, or if your son has discerned this for himself, discuss which other motor or sensory skills could be "pressed into service" to make up for the ones that are compromised by his disability.

Direct your child toward physical activities, games, and sports that will capitalize on his natural strengths

Maybe your son vowed never to get back on a soccer field again, but it doesn't mean he wouldn't enjoy going running one-on-one with you. Or Rollerblading next to you as you run. It won't be your customary five-miler, but what is it you're really trying to accomplish? Run the shorty track with your son, and do your regular run at a different time.

Does your son have a problem with fine motor coordination but not with balance? Take him sailing, kayaking, long boarding, or dirt biking. If he's got great eye-hand coordination but isn't a big fan of the outdoors, there's fencing, woodcarving, martial arts, laser tag, and Ping-Pong. Check out skeet shooting, falconry, go-karts, and billiards. You get the point. Ballplayers aren't the only ones having fun out there.

Help boys understand why their bodies won't always do what they tell them to do

Children need help making the connection between their disabilities and the challenges they encounter when playing, climbing, catching, holding, discerning distances, or balancing themselves. Left on their own by well-meaning parents worried they'll hurt their son's feelings or make him even more sensitive about the issue than he already is, these kids end up thinking the worst—that they're defective, their bodies are defective, they're stupid, they can't do anything right, they'll never be able to be like the other kids, the mean kids on the playground were right . . . Even the most bumbled conversation on the part of a parent will leave a child feeling better about himself than the (likely critical) self-talk generated in its absence. Parents of elementary-school-age kids can think about saying any of the following:

I notice when you try to play on the jungle gym/shoot baskets/tie your Rollerblades/ride your friend's scooter/play Dance Dance Revolution that it takes you a little longer to get it than some of your buddies. I've seen you get frustrated and I can totally understand why you would feel that way. There are a lot of different reasons why some kids are better at sports and moving their bodies around than others, and I want to talk with you about it so that you are aware of the types of things your body has to work extra hard to do, and the things your body is able to do well.

Everyone does some things well and nobody does everything well. Some of the reasons why certain sports or activities are easier or harder for kids have to do with the fact that our bodies are unbelievably complex. For instance, just walking involves all these different systems—your visual system and motor (muscles) system, plus your sense of balance and touch, and where your leg is in space and where it is in relation to the ground. Coordinating all that is the job of the brain, and the slightest little glitch in how messages get sent from one part of the body to another part can make a difference in how well somebody knows when to hit a Ping-Pong ball back and just how hard to hit it.

Everybody has some parts of their body that work better than others, and most of the time we don't know which parts those are because it's hard to tell what's happening on the inside—all we know is that we do some things well and other things not so well. Your mom and I notice that certain things like climbing, or running up steps, are hard for you, and it may be connected to some of the difficulties you've been having in school in some of your subjects. We're going to talk with your teachers and check that out. But the

*cool thing is that it doesn't seem to stop you from doing the things
you like doing, and we think that's great. We like that you do things
even though they're hard for you or that other kids do them better.
And while you keep doing that, we'll find out about ideas or strategies for making some of those things a little easier for you.*

Let's look at a situation in which your family goes for a day
trip to the mountains in order to learn to snowboard. Your
daughters took to it like fish to water, but your twelve-year-old
son, who loves sports but has always struggled with activities
involving gross motor control and balance, struggled through
both his lesson and his afternoon of practicing. He moped on the
drive home, declaring the day "a waste of time." Later on, or even
some other day, let him know you'd like to talk about how disappointing the day turned out for him, in order to figure out why
snowboarding was so difficult for him to learn and how to avoid
days like that in the future.

Ask your son what was different about learning to snowboard
as opposed to other physical activities or sports that have been
easier for him to learn. If you haven't already spoken with him
about his learning disabilities, and the different ways in which
they affect him, use this as an opportunity to introduce the subject; it could even provide him with some relief. Would he like
to try it again, or maybe try skiing instead? Would he prefer to
take lessons separately from his sisters? Whatever the outcome,
the most important thing is that your son knows you tried to
help him process an experience that, because of the challenges
he faces controlling his body, left him with his head hanging

pretty low. If nothing else, it keeps his disability from disappearing into the abyss of "things never to be spoken about again." It doesn't have to come up often or with any kind of regularity, but any important topic that *never* comes up between people has never really been put to rest.

Debunk the myth that "all boys play sports"

If you have a son, let him know early on that the world will think he's supposed to play sports, but that sometimes the world is wrong. By the time Jake's twin brother, Austin, was three years old, he was in love with balls of every size. When he couldn't find a conventional ball, he'd start searching for them under lamp shades, lightbulbs being the next closest thing. When he found what he thought he was looking for under those shades, he'd yell, "Ball! Ball!" with precocious glee. By age seven, he was already making his mark on the local playing fields. He had a jaunty, easy confidence, and grew popular among his peers in those early years of grade school.

Jake, however, was born with a mild muscle disorder, and lacked the physical agility, gross motor coordination, and motor strength of his handier brother. By the time they started elementary school, the divide between them with regard to athletic skill was significant. And although it had been in the making for a long time, what was different now was that *they saw it, too.*

On a night following yet another of Austin's sports victories, I decided that if I was going to help Jake develop a strong self concept, I needed to be proactive in helping him see his brother's athletic achievements as just one of the many ways in which a person can stand out or display excellence. I thought it was also important that Jake's genuine enthusiasm and pride in Austin's athletic accomplishments not be allowed to wilt in the wake of what were certain to be unavoidable comparisons by both himself and other people.

I went into Jake's room and sat on his bed while he searched around for a pair of pajamas. I told him that I thought he was a big man of a kid to continue being so proud of his brother's success in sports. I told him that children are born with different sets of talents, and some, like Austin's, show on the outside, while others, like his, show on the inside. "Austin's strengths," I said, "are the kind that other kids can see with their eyes, and they're things that seem the most important when you're five and six and seven years old." Jake's eyes met mine and I continued. "You are going to have to be very patient while waiting for your turn to shine, more patient than you should have to be. But, if you can be that patient, then when you are a little older—twelve, thirteen—the special things you have on the inside will show on the outside, too."

If you have a son, let him know early on that the world will think he's supposed to play sports, but that sometimes the world is wrong.

Helping young children to make sense of confounding experiences *as they're happening to them* can be a gift. So many parents believe that, at five and six and seven years of age, their kids are too young to understand what they would be trying to say to them. But if a child is able to detect differences between how he is treated or regarded and how other kids his age are treated, then doesn't he deserve our help in dealing with it?

Here's an example of how a father could talk sensitively with his preteenage son whose disinterest in sports might be making him worry about disappointing his dad:

Hey, dude, you and I both can see that until around the age of twelve or so, most boys connect with each other through sports. Sometimes I think about what it must be like for you to hang around other boys, because I know you're not into sports and stuff, and I think it's very hard in our society to be a boy and not like sports. I want you to know you're not alone—that there are many other boys just like you, and that I'll help you to find them. But most important, I don't ever want you to worry about disappointing me by not being a kid who's into playing football or wrestling or other things like that. Just because you see me enjoying those things doesn't mean that I expect you to. I'll be happiest seeing you doing what you love doing, whatever that turns out to be.

I remember meeting a mother who, for years, had told her slight-statured, artistically inclined son that things would get better for him once he turned twelve. And they really did. Having waded defensively through years of trying to justify his choice of nonconventional summer camps and after-school activities, Eric was finally old enough and confident enough to "own" his interests—Broadway musicals, photography, animal migration—without always feeling so self-conscious. That alone gained him the respect of his peers—a paradox understandably, albeit unfortunately, lost on most kids.

In any event, Eric's parents understood that some of the brightest parts of their son's personality were not going to be appreciated by a peer group of eight-, nine-, or ten-year-olds. And so, anticipating the social battering that Eric indeed wound up having to endure, they took measures to protect his authentic self. For years, Eric's mom and dad kept alive a vision of their son that ran alongside the one being shaped by his schoolyard interactions. Part preparation and part posthypnotic suggestion in its most artful form, they spent the first ten years of Eric's life articulating and reinforcing their truth that he was a valued and valuable member of the family and community, and that the only reason why it might not be obvious to others is that kids and even some adults will inevitably judge other kids by how closely they resemble traditional masculine ideals.

But there's another piece to this story and it's huge: Every summer, Eric's parents made a point to send him back to France, his country of origin. "For two months out of each year," his mom said, "Eric is a *normal* boy. Males are just so much more comfortable with their artistic side and their emotions than they are here in the United States. It's not so much of an either/or thing, with sports on one side and the arts on the other. Boys are boys whether or not they play rugby or box or dance. *It doesn't matter.* No one over there ever has to be a star athlete in order to be the popular kid on the block."

Europeans have always handled these matters with more grace than Americans. Their masculine icons are lithe and debonair in comparison to America's big broody kind of guy; in a sense, a lot of the boys we talk about in this book have more in common with European males than with their American brothers. It's interesting to consider the undeniably enthusiastic response on the part of American females to male Russian figure and pairs skaters whenever the winter Olympics take place. The fact that these guys skate at all only makes them more attractive, not less, reflecting the role of context in how gender conformity is perceived . Covering the 2006 winter Olympics, *Philadelphia Inquirer* sports columnist Phil Sheridan observed that Russian skaters didn't seem to wrestle at all with America's outdated ideas about masculinity that put skating in the questionable category of acceptable male sports. He added, wryly, that "[i]f any Russian tough guys are snickering, Baryshnikov and [Olympic gold medalist figure skater Evgeny] Plushenko are too busy making time with fabulous women to hear them anyway."[6]

CHAPTER THREE

The Role of Sports in Boys' Lives

A kind-looking man in his seventies joins Jake and me in an elevator. Outside, it is a spectacular spring day. The man looks over at Jake and assuming, of course, that all boys play sports, says, "It's a beautiful day for playing baseball. I bet you can't wait to get out there." Jake gazes silently at the man's face for a moment before giving him a weak smile and something that looked like a cross between a nod and a shrug.

Like 'em or not, sports will be a part of every boy's life. For those boys who enjoy and celebrate them, sports assume an easy and familiar place: after-school activity, casual interest, all-consuming passion, seasonal hobby. The boys love them, and sports love them back. Other boys have more ambivalent relationships with sports; they want to want them, but find they don't. Or they do want them, but find they aren't any good at them. These boys are interested in sports, but sports just aren't interested in them. And some boys just don't want them at all.

The exaltation of sports and their star players that we see today was seeded well over a century ago. Athletics at that time were celebrated for doing everything from siphoning off "animal spirits" to preparing young men for war to rescuing boys from the seducing "haunts of dissipation" we know today as taverns, gambling parlors, and brothels.[1] Moreover, with midnineteenth-century gender politics lending the impression that any form of male self-indulgence (material, sensual) were marks of effeminacy,[2] it's no wonder that organized sports, with their reputation for teaching self-control, were credited with turning boys into men—or at least, less like women.

Sports indeed do a lot of things. They teach teamwork, perseverance, how to perform under pressure, and, under the best of conditions and coaches, grace and generosity. Sports make muscles and lungs strong, give kids a safe place to compete with one another, and shunt off aggression from kids who are angry or frustrated and have no place to go with it. They offer camaraderie for some, a place with rules and routines for those who like their world orderly and methodical, and for yet others, a way by which to measure progress or personal transformation.

There are other specific mental and physical health benefits to sports as well. Teen athletes have been shown to have consistently higher grades, higher graduation rates, lower pregnancy rates, and lower rates of drug and alcohol abuse than their nonathletic peers,[3] though one wonders whether it is the better-supported, more internally motivated, and less impulsive adolescent who happens *also* to be a good athlete. Another important benefit—one that some parents refuse to consider—is learning how to deal with having tried and failed, or having played well but losing anyway, the value of these experiences overlooked by those who view sports only through lenses of routs and romps, crowns and laurels.

FAIL IS NOT A FOUR-LETTER WORD

Nine-year-old Billy had been a brash schoolyard basketball player when I first met him. Now, a year later, he sat in my office sad and forlorn, next to his worried dad. "He won't play basketball or do anything with the other kids," his dad said. "He just wants to play video games, and only by himself."

I remembered something else about Billy—he'd been a kid who enjoyed playing as long as he won. It wasn't that he didn't like playing if he didn't win; *he didn't play* unless he knew he was going to win.

Billy, an only child, had lost his mother to cancer when he was three years old. His paternal grandparents were helping Billy's father raise and care for Billy. Over the years, however, unable to bear the idea of Billy losing anything more, Billy's grandparents would let him win anything they could—board games, contests, arguments. Outside of his grandparents' home, however, Billy had to win the old-fashioned way, by earning it. Soon, Billy was playing only with his grandparents and father.

This is a good example of how misguided compassion can end up being a child's worst enemy in terms of healthy social and emotional development. Winning games or battles could offer only short-term gratification for a boy who would have gotten more from learning that he was a winner in his family's eyes no matter what his standings in a game were or whether they agreed or disagreed on things. In a vacuum, winning really doesn't mean a whole lot in the end. Billy had been disadvantaged by his family's sympathetic overtures—so dependent upon winning in order to feel important that he couldn't tolerate the frustration of playing with other kids and losing. And so he played alone.

The sad truth is that in the long run the world doesn't care a whole lot about any one person's pain; it keeps on spinning. But close family members and relatives and friends and others do care, and children, whether grieving, disabled, impaired or not, are best served when those around them sympathize without holding them to a lesser standard of being. Beth and I both believe very strongly that compassion is best expressed directly—through words or kind eyes or touch or simple gestures of support during unquiet moments. Saying something like, *I'm sorry that these things are difficult for you*, and *I'm so sorry that I can't give you the one thing I know you want more than anything—your mom—and it makes me want to give you everything else in this world, but I can't, and shouldn't even if I could,* do more for a child's heart and for his ability to relate genuinely and clearly with others than any material victory ever could.

According to William Pollack, however, author of *Real Boys: Rescuing Our Sons from the Myths of Boyhood,* sports do at least one thing that other activities don't: They offer an easily accessible arena in which society's traditional strictures about masculinity are loosened. It is here—on the playing field, in the locker room, on the court—that boys can show unbounded expression, and be emotionally intimate with other males. They can hug and cry and chest-bump without a moment's worth of self-consciousness. In an ironic twist that any student of male psychology could appreciate, the sporting arena, with its peddled machismo and trash talk, appears to be the only place where guys can get away with breaking Boy Code.

No wonder, then, that sport is such a vital part of male social communities. In addition, notes sociologist Michael Messner, author of "Boyhood, Organized Sports, and the Construction of Masculinity," with its clear boundaries, distance, and separations, the rule-bound structure of organized sports help guys establish parameters in their relationships with each other. To wit, consider what William Bryan, director of the Lionville Holistic Health Center and owner of Tri-Scale Massage and Bodywork, in Lionville, Pennsylvania, had to say about his male clientele:

"I can guarantee you that whenever I'm massaging a man for his first time, the topic of sports will make its appearance within the first five minutes of the hour," Bryan attested. "I think it's a test of sorts—you know, like if I can talk sports back with him, then the guy feels safe. Plus it's a boundary thing, as in, 'I'm a "real" man here, as I just made apparent by talking about sports. So, respect it, dude.'"

What happens, then, to the boys who don't have sports in their lives? Some, like Gary, a writer who all his life gravitated to the arts rather than to sports, feel as though they missed out on certain gender-based, near-universal experiences that couldn't be captured through other activities. "In all my years at school," he recounted, "I was never once part of a team. I liked being independent, accountable only to myself. If I messed up, it was on me and only me. I didn't have to deal with feeling that I'd let others down. But now of course I realize I did myself a disservice. I never got used to having people count on me." Gary paused for a moment before ending with, "I guess I feel as though I missed out on some sort of socialization process, and never really caught up."

Craig, a high school science teacher in his midforties, felt similarly to Gary—that he'd lost out on something important by not playing on a sports team. But while, for Gary, it was the opportunity to become comfortable in roles where he would have had to be accountable to his peers, Craig missed the distinctive kind of social climate he believes develops among boys who play together on teams. "The problem," said Craig, "was that you missed out on the camaraderie, on the feeling of belonging to a big club. When I was growing up, there were few alternatives to sports for boys, so if you didn't get it there, you didn't get it, period. Now at least you can get that by joining chorus, or one of the community service clubs. But then again, there's something about competition that creates a climate that just doesn't happen when you're not competing. It's like you're all fighting for something together. It's different. I never got anything close to that in any of the couple of clubs I joined in middle school and high school."

As Craig hinted at, boys who don't conform to the brawny roles they're expected to play sometimes do have to work harder than other boys at finding social and recreational networks that suit their personality and interests, though less so now than in the past. The type of community in which you're raised makes a difference, too. Boys who grow up in urban, diversity-friendly cities will fare better than those being raised in homogeneous towns where exposure to different people and perspectives is more limited. And with their healthy economic bases and more fully endowed school districts, many of the suburbs surrounding thriving metropolitan cities are also in a strong position to offer their young constituents alternatives to the standard set of sports and hobbies. Boys living in such places have music education in the schools, chess clubs, robotics, and archery. They have opportunities to learn how to fence, act, cook, and video-edit, and follow it all up with camps that teach them what emergency medical technicians do on the job or how astronauts train for missions. Being a kid who doesn't "fit in" is a whole lot more manageable when you're not the only one, and there are a lot of things for you to do.

Just look at what Billy Elliot endured, in the movie of the same name. Growing up in an English mining town a long way from London, eleven-year-old Billy first had to hide, and then was berated for, his love of dancing—ballet no less. Eventually Billy's resolve breaks through the staunch prejudice of his dad, older brother, and fellow townsmen, but only after Billy spends a half year dancing again in secrecy, and only after his ballet instructor bravely goes toe-to-toe with his dad and brother on Billy's behalf, and only after the men become mesmerized by Billy's talent and his transcendent joy in dancing.

Billy, however, had some things going for him that other boys pursuing unconventional recreation may not. He had drive, a plucky dance teacher, and a father who could be emotionally moved by the power and grace of his son's dancing. In reality, a lot of kids go it alone.

That's especially true for boys living in more rural or economically challenged cities and towns. Fewer resources mean that the schools, which are largely responsible for recreational programming, are likely going to stick to a more traditional palette of offerings—baseball, wrestling, football, basketball, and the like. Messner also points out that in working-class communities especially, sports are *the* place for boys to make their mark. Sometimes it's the only visible way out of the neighborhood and to a better life. How does a boy who lives here, and who's disinterested in sports, establish some kind of personal and social presence?

I am reminded of Gordy's sad plight in *Stand by Me*, the 1986 coming-of-age movie about four boys on the cusp of adolescence. On an adventure away from home, Gordy is sent by his three friends to a corner market to get some food. A scene shows him standing, bewildered and forlorn, in the back of the store, looking for something he could buy with the few cents he and his friends have pooled. The store clerk looks over at the boy, who brings to his mind Gordy's older brother, the football hero and shining star in this small town who had died in an accident a few years back.

> "You're asking for a hated son! Lads do football or boxing or wrestling—not ballet."
>
> Billy Elliot's father, upon finding out that Billy had been taking dance lessons instead of boxing lessons, and being told by his son that he wasn't giving them up, in the movie *Billy Elliot*

"Do you play football?" the man behind the counter asks. There was only one right answer.

"No," Gordy replies.

"What do you do, then?"

Gordy turns to look at the clerk. "I don't know," is all he says.

Is there a qualitative difference between the kind of camaraderie that develops among boys on competitive sports teams and what you find among those in other, even tightly knit, social groups?

Maybe there is. Maybe there's something about the physicality of the experience, the risk of injury and collection of war bruises, and the mission of fighting for something together that galvanizes the group in a way that just feels different. It's what comes to mind when I hear people suggest that a boy who isn't interested in sports can look toward such activities as debate team in order to experience competition as well as teamwork. It's a good idea—as long as we're not pretending that one substitutes for the other. They are different experiences, even different competitive experiences, for different sets of boys.

My three boys go to summer camp for seven weeks and spend five of the days engrossed in Color War, which is nothing but competition and teamwork. All three say it's their favorite five days of camp, including Jake. My friend's kids don't go to summer camp but, instead, spend a few weeks every year visiting relatives in Spain. They wouldn't consider trading their time in Spain for somewhere else any more than my kids would consider skipping a year of camp. As a parent, I consider the years that my boys have spent at summer camp to have been not only irreplaceable, but downright indispensable, in terms of their personal growth. But in the parallel universes of other parents' perspectives, some of the experiences that their kids have had, and mine have not, are the ones deemed indispensable. It doesn't matter. We all use what we have and what we're given, and make meaning of it later. Experiences are seen as indispensable or irreplaceable only *after* a person's had them. Until then, the possibilities for such remain grand, and largely unknowable.

Being part of a sports team may not be able to be replicated in full by other, nonathletic experiences. *But it doesn't have to be.* With the exception perhaps of the intense camaraderie, fortified no doubt by physically "conquering" a common enemy, I think that a lot of what sports offer boys is neither limited to athletics nor indispensable. Teamwork and perseverance are a part of any science-fair project, wind ensemble, or group of kids trying to raise money for a good cause. Grace and generosity can be taught in as banal a venue as the grocery store, where we teach our children to wait patiently as a single mother with three restless kids tries to write out a check in between attempts to shepherd her crew. Walking to school, filling water buckets for the animals in the barn, and chopping lumber at a wolf refuge to erect shelters build strong muscles and lungs, too.

Sports and Status: Reducing "Jock Domination"

By now, it should hardly be surprising that a 1999 national telephone survey by ESPN found that nearly three-quarters of high school students noticed some level of tension between athletes and nonathletes in their school. Apparently, all that earlier schoolyard jostling for position was just a foreshadowing for what was to come. "They walk around like they own the place," says high school sophomore Jonathan, in an article about "jock privilege" published by Teaching Tolerance, a project of the Southern

"JOCKOCRACY"

A scholastic environment . . . where sports/athletics are placed as the highest priority of education above all others. Sports/athletic participants are viewed, by those in charge, as the greatest heroes of this environment. They are usually aware of this, and take unfair advantage of it, usually exerting unfair influence on *nonjocks,* and nonathletic instructors. Often, they get away with this more freely than others would, dragging down the actual educational standards of the entire institution.[4]

Poverty Law Center in Montgomery, Alabama. "Sometimes you'll be walking in the hall, and one of the football guys will bump into you. Or you'll be hanging out in the cafeteria, and they'll make fun of your clothes real loud, because they know that they're stronger and more popular."[5]

In the same article, University of Colorado sociology professor Jay Coakley's observations about athletes who exploit their status in school support the experiences reported by Jonathan. In describing how these athletes hold themselves out as separate from the rest of the student body, claiming extra privileges in the process, Coakley says, "Because of the attention being paid to their sports, those student athletes sometimes feel they have permission to dominate the social organization of the school. They do that in a variety of ways, usually claiming space in hallways and in cafeteria lines, and taking opportunities in some cases to demean other students, enhancing their own status in the process." Elaborating on this relationship between sport status and power, Carol Lieber, director for secondary programs for Educators for Social Responsibility, comments on the extra leverage provided by playing varsity sports in particular, saying, "Males who participate in activities like football and wrestling tend to dominate high school cultures, both physically and socially. These things determine who feels they have a voice that matters. In some cases, those who feel privileged abuse others."[6]

However, some educators, recognizing the enormous social influence wielded by their star team players, feel a sense of responsibility to mitigate the divisiveness it breeds. The prominence of his football team in the community of Odessa, Texas, led Permian High School head coach T. J. Mills to incorporate thirty-minute "character development" lessons into his football training sessions to discuss life *off* the field. "Football has been a way of life in Odessa for decades," said Mills. "That gives us a special responsibility to make sure that we keep our players acting the right way and setting a good example. We have to be more diligent than a lot of other schools in making sure our players aren't harassing other kids."[7]

Mark Calhoun, math teacher and head football coach at Denver's East High, affirms the idea that there are social responsibilities associated with certain coaching positions. "I get concerned that football players can be bullies," he says, "so I talk to my team about it." In addition, Calhoun encourages his football players to join other school activities, an uncommon policy among high school coaches. He likes that his players will gain skills not necessarily garnered from sports, as well as have opportunities to develop a respect for the efforts of kids involved in nonathletic activities. With his football players on the speech team and in the school musicals, Calhoun has helped make the concept of crossover athletes a reality.

But opportunities for drama students to go to sporting events and athletes to go to art functions won't appear by themselves. "[T]hese things don't happen by accident," cautions Lieber, and she's right. Schools need the support of teachers and the active interest of enough students to create a tipping point, where the idea of desegregating the "jocks" and "nonjocks"—something many in the school might have thought of as idealistic or irrelevant—finally "takes" and is implemented.

Whimsy and creativity can help grease the wheels of change here and schools will need it; getting students to alter their social patterns is never a simple feat. I'm talking about the freshman baseball team inviting the photography club to do a food drive for Thanksgiving. Or the wind ensemble challenging the wrestling team to a nerf-ball match. Or the boys cross-country team and National Honor Society holding a fund-raising car wash together. By "playing" with long-standing issues that no one ever comes out and identifies but that everyone recognizes, school communities can finally make overt some of the covert competitiveness undermining their social climates. Because, inevitably, in the light of day and under the scrutiny of mutual awareness, the dynamics supporting condescension and power plays between people are more easily disabled. Maybe by pushing football fields and baseball diamonds to share the stage with other venues for self-development and expression, the cultures at schools fostering caste systems can, finally, begin to be changed.

Classroom teachers, too, can play big roles in shifting school cultures away from those of athletic privilege toward those of equity. Coakley remarks that the breaks and preferential treatment sometimes given to athletes by teachers relates to their seeing sports participation as worthwhile, and indicative of positive traits. That's fine, but why the exemption for sports participants only? We know that other students invest productively in a wide variety of activities, exercising their qualities of responsibility, initiative, creativity, and leadership. In teachers' defense, though, Coakley points out that they may be better able to recognize the demands on athletes' schedules than on the schedules of other students whose commitments are invisible to the school community—after-school jobs, off-site activities (elite dancing or skating; religious youth and service groups), or responsibilities to care for siblings or an ill parent at home. He adds that students shine when given opportunities to try hard, support each other, and receive adult encouragement. "If we treated all students the way we treat student athletes," says Coakley, "we'd have a lot fewer problems and a lot better schools."

BRIDGING THE DIVIDE BETWEEN ATHLETES AND THEIR NONATHLETIC PEERS

- Coaches should encourage students to participate in school activities and clubs other than their respective sport(s). With a little flexibility and, for some coaches, a less grandiose sense of purpose, most minor or occasional schedule conflicts can be worked out. A ninth grader in therapy with me was delighted to play on her first school sport team only to be forced by her new coach to choose between being on the team and participating in the school play. There would have been a period of four weeks where practice and rehearsal schedules overlapped, for one day a week only. You'd think this would have been a manageable problem. When coaches take themselves and their athletic missions too seriously, demanding exclusivity or mandating attendance during holiday breaks and benching kids whose families follow through with long-standing vacation plans, school sports become a caricature of what they're supposed to be. The girl chose the play, by the way, and hasn't touched another sport since.

- In schools where the issue of jock domination has had a noticeably divisive effect, teachers or student councils could assign a small group of "volunteer liaisons," whose role would be to collect and implement ideas for creating bridges between these groups of students. Some people worry that identifying and putting a spotlight on a problem like this makes it a bigger one, and it could, if the thrust behind it came from administration and parents. Students then would likely feel imposed upon, forced to respond to an agenda that wasn't theirs. This kind of project works only if it matters at least as much to the student body as it does to others who are helping it along. Part of the groundwork here may then need to be getting kids talking about and answering this question: Why should it matter that the kids who are really into sports and the kids who aren't get along? What difference will this make in my experience of high school?

- Parents can encourage their children's schools to offer activities that are "sporty" but also playful (extreme pogo sticking), novel (fencing), or physical in nature and outcome-oriented but unlike traditional sports. These kinds of things would be terrific additions to the usual array of offerings having typically to do with balls.

Athletics and Scholarship: A Spurious Divide

Brainy boys have a long history of being thought of as unathletic. You're either a geek *or* a jock, the concept of dual talenthood lost on those who see things in terms of either/or rather than both/and. In their book *Smart Boys: Talent, Manhood, and the Search for*

Meaning, psychologists Barbara A. Kerr and Sanford J. Cohn examined the specific social challenges faced by intellectually gifted girls and boys, and found that the unathletic boys are quickly rejected by other boys. They also discovered that gifted boys are considered, of all things, "boring." Kerr and Cohn concluded that our culture's ideals of masculinity, stressing physical agility over intelligence, compel smart boys and men "to ignore the urgings of their intellect and creative selves in order to fulfill socially ordained masculine roles."

> "Gifted boys learn very early that if they are smart, they had better be smart and athletic; athletic ability makes intelligence acceptable."
>
> Barbara Kerr

These stereotypes are proving very costly: More and more boys, anxious about their perceived masculinity, hide their intellectual giftedness and become "closet" intellectuals. In a 2000 keynote speech about genius and gender, Barbara Kerr stated, "Gifted boys learn very early that if they are smart, they had better be smart and athletic; athletic ability makes intelligence acceptable."[8] Kerr added, "The non-athletic gifted boy is doomed to social rejection . . . *unless he discovers a special talent for underachievement* [italics mine]." Underachieving, Kerr explains, has become a way for boys to assert their independence and masculinity and, especially in classrooms where girls are excelling and the teacher is female, separate themselves from the girls. It's sort of a double whammy for intelligent nonathletic boys: They can't (or don't want to) do the thing that makes boys popular, and can do the thing that gets in its way.

This puzzling pattern of behavior—feigning academic indifference—shows up as early as elementary school. Kerr and colleague Megan Nicpon call it the "Bartleby syndrome"[9]—symptoms of the "intellectual death" suffered by many gifted boys in the later elementary school grades, when they learn that "it isn't cool to be the best student in class."[10] *Time* magazine columnist Joel Stein simply calls it "nerdophobia."

Thirteen-year-old Sean was a casualty of this prejudice against boys who are both nonathletic and smart. He had a nimble and versatile intellect, but instead of celebrating his intelligence, he tried to hide it. "He loves to play chess but won't join the chess club at school because he doesn't want to be identified as one of 'those' kids," said his mother, Wendy. "He won an award at school for academic excellence but came close to refusing to go to the ceremony. But what really broke my heart was when he told his dad, whose three siblings went to college on full athletic scholarships, that he felt he was a *disappointment* to us because he was never going to be able to do that." With tears in her eyes, Wendy said to me, "My son worries about being a disappointment to his parents because all he can do is be smart."

I once stood and listened to a mother talk at length to an acquaintance about her son's most recent athletic achievements and the accolades he'd received from his coaches. The friend listened with interest. So I ran a little experiment in my head and imagined the mother instead talking up her son's most recent academic achievements for the same length of time. In this brief fantasy, the friend's reaction to the mother was different: *Wow, does she think she's the only mother with a smart kid?*

BE SMART OR BE COOL?

Some boys who don't play sports feel
they have to choose one over the other.

CONVERSATION STARTER FOR PARENTS

Introduce at home the topic of "social cultures" in language your young son can understand. Ask him if it's cool or not cool to be smart in his school. Tell him you've heard that some kids in middle school think it's not cool to be smart and try to hide it from their classmates. Ask him if he ever felt like hiding how much he knew about a topic, or how well he had studied for an exam.

Tell him the story about the kid who was really good at chess but was embarrassed to play at school for fear of being teased. Ask him if he knows of anyone in his school who has done something like that. What would he do if he was really good at chess and there was this club at his school but the kids who played in the club got teased?

The purpose here isn't to resolve the problem in that moment, but rather to embark on a dialogue with your son that can be carried through over time.

If your son is one of those kids who downplays his intelligence whenever he's in front of his friends, think about when and where you could bring up something about how you've been hearing that some boys don't like other kids to know how smart they are. If you start right off by asking your son if he does that, the conversation probably won't get very far. But by first "normalizing" the behavior, i.e., mentioning you've heard that a lot of boys worry about looking too smart and being teased, you make it easier for him to, eventually, talk about it himself (though it may come by way of "other kids" he knows who do that) or let you lead a conversation about it, with him joining in here and there.

Now, it's very likely that your son will respond by saying that's the stupidest thing he's ever heard, that nobody pretends to be dumber than they are. It's fine. There's no argument. The point isn't to have him agree. Just respond with a casual (but not critical or dismissive) shrug of your shoulders, and something like, *Yeah, well, it does sound kind of odd but, actually, I think they may be right. And to be totally honest with you, sometimes I think I notice you doing that around your friends.* And when your son says, *What are you talking about?!* you can respond with, *I don't know, it's just that when you're around your friends, especially your guy friends, you don't talk the way you usually do. I don't know how to explain it, it's just different, as if you don't want them to see that you're a smart kid . . .* Then let it rest. Go on to something else (unless of course your son wants to talk about it some more). That way he'll understand you're not trying to prove you're right or "get" him to change. People need time to make those types of changes anyway; it's not really a "decision" you make. Revisit the whole thing another day. All you're trying to do now is prompt your son to think about this idea in relation to himself, which is how change can begin in someone who wasn't looking for it in the first place.

Maybe in our culture it's simply more acceptable to casually boast about your children's athletic achievements than their scholastic achievements. *Hey, he won his match today!* sounds better than *My son just scored 2200 on his SATs!* Americans champion the value of education and academic excellence, but it seems that of the countless conversations parents have about their own and each other's kids, I'd bet the majority have more to do with who's shining on the lacrosse fields and tennis courts than with who's shining in the classroom.

HELPING KIDS LEARN TO VALUE THEIR INTELLECT AND EDUCATION

DOING SOMETHING DIFFERENT AT HOME...

If you discover that being smart or educated is not valued by your child's peer group at school, then make a point to value it more visibly at home.

Keep the matter light, so your kids don't brace against conversations you might try to start about the books or movies you love, or about interesting current events. Switch things around on family movie night and bring out one of the wordplay board games stuffed in the back of a closet. Just be sure to play one that *you* actually like so that it doesn't feel forced or contrived. That's the best way for your kids to get past any cynicism they might have, and actually find themselves getting interested in playing themselves. If they say they're too old for board games, pitch it as a competition, or even as "crosstraining." After all, a lot of winning in sports can indeed be attributed to a player's skill in handling the mental game.

One more thing—unless your children are very young, be careful not to artificially simplify your vocabulary or limit the breadth of topics (unless inappropriate) when you talk with your kids or with another adult in your kids' presence. Children are intrigued when they hear their parents offer up well-articulated opinions or insightful remarks that reveal an active, hungry intellect behind the voice they more commonly hear saying, *What time should I pick you up?* or *It's time to get off the computer* or even *Love you, baby!* I'm not talking about pedantic lectures at the dinner table that some parents try to pass off as "quality family time." I'm talking about the bits and pieces of conversation and commentary and reflection that emerge from our everyday interactions and reveal who we are *as individuals apart from our role as parents*—one of the best ways, as far as I'm concerned, to remain a relevant and compelling figure to your children long after their launch into adulthood.

This irony in the American attitude toward education is exactly what author Avi Wortel intended to portray in *S.O.R. Losers,* his young-adult novel about a group of unathletic boys forced by their school to form a soccer team. "On the one hand," Wortel notes, "our culture likes to give a lot of lip service to support for kids, but on the other hand, I don't think the culture as a whole likes kids. And kids are caught in this contradiction. I ask teachers at conferences 'How many of you have athletic trophies displayed at your schools?' You know how many raise their hands. And I ask 'How many of you have trophy displays for the best reader or writer?' Nobody raises their hands. And I say 'What is it therefore that stands out as the essential achievement in your school?' With test scores falling, we need to make kids better readers, but instead we're interested in a minority of kids, mostly males, whose primary focus is sports."

> "The ones we need to be celebrating aren't the winners of the Super Bowl but the winners of the Science Fair."
>
> President Barack Obama, State of the Union Address, January 2011

"Just look at the messages kids are getting from their own schools," says Bryan, the holistic massage therapist from earlier in the chapter, reinforcing Wortel's point. "High schools deflect money from music or art programs all the time. Students know where the money goes, and it's definitely not to improve the music program. It goes to athletics. And guess which students are getting the biggest scholarships? It's the star athletes. High schools prep their students specifically for that. Athletics is just a much bigger industry."

Bryan isn't kidding. From the moment the new generation of five- and six-year-old kids first start suiting up for their soccer matches, they are learning just how much a slick kick into the net or a good block is worth to their teammates, coach, and parents. And it continues to build from there. Schools are often rated on how many scholarships their students are offered, and this encourages them to invest heavily in those students who are seen as more likely to win them—namely, athletes. In an article about the activities and personal characteristics that college admissions currently value most highly, college consultant Estee Pickens noted that even during this time of record-breaking selectivity at our nation's schools, talented athletes are in high demand.[11] "The stakes associated with varsity programs have become greater," observed the University of Colorado's Coakley. "Athletes are being heavily recruited and publicized; some are even jumping straight into professional sports from the high school level. In fact, three of the four top picks in the last National Basketball Association draft were high school seniors. They're being covered in more newspapers and even getting television exposure. They've also seen a proliferation of Web sites and booster clubs that make them more visible in the community."[12] Laments Bryan, "What a perfect setup for a boy who's not into sports to spend his academic career feeling like a second-class citizen."

"Using athletics as a sole barometer of masculinity is a major problem," concluded Bryan. "Everyone needs to have a sense of place in their community, a location where they are recognized, where they feel they fit in. Athletics speak the language of 'place'—you're either first or second or third or last . . . But if you

SHOWCASING STUDENTS WHO CONTRIBUTE IN AREAS OTHER THAN ATHLETICS

DOING SOMETHING DIFFERENT IN THE SCHOOLS . . .

Generate publicity for a wider range of school-based activities—the ones that do not get much attention. Use morning announcements, the school paper, and the school's website to publicize which kid won an essay contest, how the band did at regionals, or who was voted president of the debate team. These are names that too few students or teachers ever hear, yet they represent active, contributing members of the school community.

Schools can be encouraged to offer awards to students who make significant contributions to the community, and open up opportunities where the student body can hear about the kinds of projects and organizations that exist. Teachers of just about any subject taught in high school can invite students to utilize any volunteer experiences they've had in one or two of their class assignments. In addition, they can try to weave themes of service, social activism, civic-mindedness, and globalism into the curriculum as much as is realistic given the volume of material they're expected to cover every year.

Put some kids in charge of developing a schoolwide or community-wide PR campaign for the arts, science, and math. It would make a terrific community or graduation project for a high school student or senior Girl/Boy Scout.

Build partnerships with business and community leaders who are in positions to offer students unique service or internship opportunities, as well as more visible platforms for recognition.

Emphasize the value of cultivating this arm of student education and personal development at school-board and home-and-school association meetings. Set up a table on Back-to-School Night hosted by kids whose enthusiasm for their engagement in the community is too inviting for parents to pass by without noticing. Encourage them to post oversize photos of different sites, show video clips of themselves in action, tell inspiring stories. Ask local psychologists and pediatricians to come speak at the school about the importance of developing the *whole* child.

give people only one place that matters, and narrow the parameters by making physical attributes the determining factor of place, then people are going to be sent scrambling, asking themselves, 'Where do I fit in?'"

Bryan makes a good point here. Sports, more than most other activities, are about rankings: who is faster or better than whom. But there are still many non-sport-related activities that rank their players and members and aficionados: There are first and second violin chairs, and lead roles versus chorus roles, and winners in everything from poetry contests to agricultural fairs. It's one of the ways by which we order the world and function within it. There are also people in this world for whom everything is a contest—jobs, cars, clothing, partners, brains, virtue—and they never cease looking over their shoulders to see who's watching.

Winning, however, can mean different things to different people, depending on what it is you won. But uncoupling the win from the rankings clears the way for more than one person to come out ahead, and that's just what happens when a person's value is measured not so much by what they do, but by who they are. In that kind of situation, one wins simply by having been *present*.

CHAPTER FOUR

Fake It, Make It— or Break

Short, stocky, and muscular in build, ten-year-old Cody was the kind of boy you take one look at and think . . . *budding wrestler*. No whistles and mats for him, though—what Cody really liked was catching, observing, and studying butterflies, a pastime not shared by his peers. Cody loved learning but hated going to school, where he had a few acquaintances but no real friends. He wore a silent question mark on his forehead throughout the day, as if trying to discern the rules of a game he was living out but couldn't comprehend. That, plus his serious demeanor, his shyness, and his lack of humor, made it difficult for other kids to approach him. Without a game of tag or kickball to break the ice, time spent around other kids felt long and lonely to Cody. By the time I was asked to see him for an evaluation of his "social problems," he was a sad boy who kept pretty much to himself.

My first impression of Cody was that he was a little man tucked into a kid's body. He was exceedingly polite and never spoke out of turn. He answered every question earnestly. In fact, it turned out that Cody himself had been the one to ask for therapy. He wanted to talk to someone about the anxiety he felt in the mornings before school, and what he could do about feeling so different from the other boys in his grade. "I don't get teased or anything," Cody explained during his first appointment. "I mean, I get along with them okay. It's just that we really don't like any of the same things. I don't let them know that, though."

"How have you managed to do that?" I asked him.

Cody pulled his gaze up from the floor and looked me square in the eye. "I fake it pretty good. I fake it *every single day*."

Faking it, in Cody's case, meant maintaining a public self that was different from his private self. Kids who fake it don't believe they can afford to let other kids know what they really think or feel, or what they truly want or like or value. They worry about the social costs of revealing something about themselves that other kids would find weird or dumb. What they're not aware of, though, are the emotional costs of keeping their genuine selves hidden from view. Research shows that kids who maintain separate private and public selves are vulnerable to depression, as well as to impulsive and compulsive behaviors, such as substance abuse, unsafe sex, and suicide threats.

There are kids who go on for years faking it without their parents ever knowing. Cody's parents, for example, sharp and well educated, were clueless about their son's split-screen life. They saw

TALKING TO BOYS WHO FEEL THEY HAVE TO FAKE LIKING SPORTS . . .

Because the pressure to conform to the peer group is so strong in children, many become adept at hiding their real selves. How much of the time, or with which people, might your own son be "faking it"? Ask him. Let him know you've noticed him trying to adapt to a social environment that expects him to like sports.

You can try saying . . .

Sometimes I wonder if what you show us on the outside is what you feel on the inside. I know that kids think boys are supposed to like playing rough sports and all, and that if you're a boy who doesn't like that, then kids think there's something the matter. You don't like rough sports, yet I see you talk to the other kids as if you do like them. So I guess I worry that you feel you have to fake it, you know, like you can't let them know the truth . . .

If your son tells you in so many words that you're right, then let him know that you appreciate how much effort it takes to keep up the facade, and that you hope as he gets a little older, he won't feel such a need to hide his real preferences. Explain to him that while most boys will always love their sports, they learn over time to love other things just as much. At that point, there will be less need for anyone to fake anything. Mention things you think might help—taking lessons in an activity he does like, exploring new activities he hasn't been exposed to yet, discovering other ways that he can feel "tough" besides pretending to like rough sports or contact sports. I once read a beautiful account of a father who quenched his young, outlaw-wannabe son's thirst for toy guns and holsters and swords with a fireman's costume and the most lifelike accoutrements he could find—breathing masks from the local hardware store, make-believe air tanks, and big, heavy garden hoses and ladders the boy could safely climb. There are a lot of ways for boys to feel strong and powerful and heroic.

Don't be offended or angry with your son if he ignores what you're saying, or looks at you as if you have no idea what you're talking about. If he gets defensive, tell him that you don't mean to put him on the spot, and don't want to make him uncomfortable. Avoid saying things like, *Well, I'm asking you these things for your own good,* or, *Fine, have it your way.* Simply move off the subject for now with a wave of your hand and comment that says it was just a thought. You can always try again later. Avoid pressing; trying to muscle your point across will only make your son resist whatever you're wanting him to see. Think of getting a response, or of exchanging thoughts about the subject, as the end goal; for right now you're just trying to let your son know that you notice—or at least think you notice—things about him that make you want to know more about what he's thinking and feeling. It's really an expression of care, above anything else.

If your son looks over at you and shrugs, consider that his way of saying, *Yeah, that's kind of true, but I'll need your help talking about this . . .* to which you can reply, *Hey, we can talk about this some more if you'd like. I'll help you, because I know it's the sort of stuff that's hard to talk about. I guess I just don't want you to always feel that you have to pretend to like something you don't, or act like someone you're not . . .* If he looks away and shrugs, he may be too embarrassed to talk about it with you, and you can let him know you'd like to at some point but that you're not in any rush.

him as a solemn kid, in need of friends, and maybe a little "adultified," but they had no idea how hard he worked to stay on this side of the divide between kids who were accepted by the peer group and those who weren't.

One reason why kids who fake it go undetected for so long appears to be the same reason why so many parents of teenagers are blindsided by problems they never suspected their kid of having: Parents tend not to scratch a surface that looks good *enough*. "He does all right in school, and has the same couple of friends he's always had," said Rich about his fifteen-year-old son, Zachary, whose school requested that he be evaluated by a psychologist. "Zach doesn't tell me all that much, but I never thought of him as in any kind of trouble or anything. He's against drugs, and I've never caught him drinking. He can get a little mouthy around the house, and he's moody a lot of the time, but his mother and I just figured it was just part of being a normal teenager."

Looking past Zachary's glib exterior, however, the school saw a boy with a disarming predilection for provoking teachers with his smarmy condescension and unbridled sarcasm. Even Zachary's demeanor was off-putting. His eye contact was protracted and felt aggressive to some of his teachers. He also took liberties with personal-space boundaries that were too brief and subtle to ever call him on, e.g., standing a little too close to people when speaking with them. The one time Zachary's school administration was able to call him out was when Zachary let himself get bent out of shape enough to actually threaten another student. He knew immediately that he'd made a mistake, but it was too late. In order to return to school, Zachary needed to get green-lighted by a mental health professional.

"This kid flies beneath his parents' radar because his problems aren't the ones that scare moms and dads," Zachary's school counselor said to me. "The ones that really get their attention are drugs, alcohol, trouble with the law, or a truant officer knocking at their front door. That's why so many parents are surprised when we call to tell them their supposedly 'good' kid isn't doing so well after all."

It would have been the same situation with Cody. As far as his parents were concerned, their son was simply having some difficulties making friends. They thought it was because he was shy. They had no idea how hard he worked every single day just to get through "undetected." Parents of younger kids don't have the veil of adolescence to rationalize away any unsettling behaviors. But that doesn't mean they don't find plausible reasons for why their child doesn't respond promptly to redirection or ever

OBSERVING YOUR SON'S SOCIAL BEHAVIORS
MORE OBJECTIVELY . . .

Try to observe your son's interactions with peers and adults as objectively as possible, without rationalizing them or finding excuses for things you see but don't like. What are your first reactions to what you see or hear? Do you find his behavior appealing and considerate, or instead, maybe pushy, immature, overly mature, attention getting, or even a little annoying? Remember that he has to live in a world that will react to him a lot less generously than his parents will. Help him adjust to that reality before he's made habits out of behaviors that could put other people off, or before he's on his own and has to figure it out for himself.

have anything nice to say to his siblings. *He's got ADD,* they'll explain, forgetting to make the distinction between inattentiveness and frank disregard.

"I just thought he was shy," said Helen, whose son, nine-year-old Justin, had begun having anxiety attacks on Sunday nights, one month after moving to a new town. "I knew he was nervous about changing schools, but I figured he'd be okay once he got to know some of the kids." Helen was probably correct about Justin's ability to adjust over time, but what she wasn't taking into account was *how much longer* it might take him, a boy with a small body frame and a circumspect personality, to find his place in a new school than the next boy, who, chances are, would use physical games or casual sports to get to know his classmates.

I asked Helen if she thought Justin's disinterest in sports could be making it harder for him to make friends at his new school. "Yes, probably," she replied, "but I wouldn't ever say anything to him about it." I asked her why not. "Well, because I wouldn't want him to feel bad about it or think that I was criticizing him for not being into the whole sports scene." Helen explained that Justin's dad was a pretty big sports fan, and had started grooming Justin to be the athlete that he himself had been in college. Justin obliged as best he could until his parents' divorce and his dad's transfer to another city six hours away relieved him of the burden of having to fake being a happy jock.

I shared with Helen my belief that her talking with Justin about being a boy who doesn't care too much for sports and roughhousing could be very helpful to him. She looked surprised, and even a little nervous.

"You've got to figure it's something he thinks about," I said, "but if no one is talking about it with him, it means he's having to think about it by himself. And at nine years old, he's not going to have the perspective he needs to see that he is bigger than the number of sports he plays. You really can talk about this with him without sounding as if you think he should be any different. In fact, I'd start the whole conversation by telling him it was your fear he would think you were criticizing him that kept you from talking about this in the first place."

"I don't know what I'd be trying to say," Helen replied. "Besides, I always figured sports were something his dad would talk to him about."

"You're not really talking to him about sports—not that you shouldn't just because his dad is," I said. "You'd be talking to Justin about himself and about going to a new school and about the fact that you wonder if being a boy who doesn't particularly like a lot of sports makes it harder for him to feel like he fits in."

"What if he just looks at me and doesn't say anything?"

"Then just smile or touch his hand or something. He doesn't have to say anything in response. Tell him these were some things you'd been thinking about and you wanted to see if he was thinking about them, too. Now that you've opened the door, he'll bring the topic up again if he feels like it. But also let Justin know that until he starts feeling a little more settled at school, you'll help him find some ways to make the adjustment period a little more manageable. Get him hooked up with his counselor and find out if he would be allowed to touch base with him or her during the school day. See if there's a Big Buddy program for new students. Maybe there's an event you can volunteer for that involves parents and their kids together. Not only would you be serving as a role model for Justin in dealing with situations where you don't know anyone, there might be opportunities to subtly facilitate some kid-to-kid contact."

Probably the hardest thing for parents to consider doing is talking to their child about something as sensitive as their personality. Instinct tells us to protect our child's feelings, to help him focus on what's positive, and on what people enjoy about him. Those things are good, too, of course, but avoiding talking to children about the things they do that may offend or impose unnecessarily on friends or family members or teachers won't help them develop self-awareness or a sensitivity toward the impact of their behaviors on other people. The common assumption is that "these things" don't need to be talked about—but they do. *Because when no one makes them part of a conversation that feels good, they will be left being associated with feeling bad or being criticized or judged.*

CONVERSATION FOR CONNECTION

So much of the conversation between parents and their children is casual or practical in nature. Only infrequently, and then often accompanied by some degree of awkwardness, do parents and kids converse for the sake of being better known to each other or understood. Think about how you might begin talking to your son about the things you think are troubling him—not for purposes of getting him to change, but simply to hear what he has to say. When kids realize that revealing things about themselves won't be taken as a sign that they're seeking advice, they become less vigilant about what they disclose.

If, while you're talking, you start feeling self-conscious, tell your son so. This will immediately take your anxiety level down and remove the need to hide from him what it is you're feeling.

You can say . . .

You know, we never talk like this. It's weird but in a good kind of way. I feel really self-conscious but I also kind of don't care!

If your son starts to look embarrassed or uncomfortable, then say something about that. It's better than leaving him to feel as if *he* now has to hide how he feels from you.

You can say . . .

I can tell you're thinking, "What is my mom up to? This is so weird . . ." It's just that I don't want to spend the next ten years feeling as if I can only ask you about how you did on your history test or what time I'm supposed to pick you up today.

It's okay if you can't think of what to say next and the conversation stops dead in its tracks. Address it directly.

You can say . . .

Not bad for two beginners, or, *I have no idea what else to say but I like what we've done so far . . .*

"I'm still faking it," remarked Alan, the optometrist whose memory of not being able to climb the rope in gym endures in spite of the passing of four decades. "I keep up with sports news just so I can fit in and have something to say. I know there are other guys who do the same thing, but you never know who's for real and who's just trying to get by. I'll be at a party and notice that some guy I know only casually isn't watching the game.

That'll be the first time I realize he's not into sports, and I'm totally surprised. And it's like, there's this instant bond. And then there are other times when I arrive at a party and see everyone gathered around the TV and think to myself, 'Damn, it looks like I came too early. I meant to miss this game.'"

Some guys never get over the feeling of needing to keep up the pretense of liking sports. Sadly, despite having become a successful attorney and noted philanthropist, forty-eight-year-old Dean felt as if he still fell short of being one of the guys. No matter what he did, it wasn't enough, because it wasn't something he had accomplished on the playing field. "I still feel as if I have to know who won last night's game and who's about to be traded," Dean said. "In some ways, I guess I feel I'm still that impostor kid."

Making It

"'You take him!' 'No, you!' 'Look, you take him and we'll give you Bobby.' 'Okay, it's a deal.' No one wanted me. That how I remember recess," said Lionville, Pennsylvania, Holistic Health Center director and massage therapist William Bryan, whom we first met in Chapter Three. I asked Bill how he managed to rise above these kinds of childhood experiences to become the congenial, confident man he now is, and he responded by telling a story.

"I remember being in sixth grade, and I was invited to a friend's birthday party. This guy's dad was so strict, I swear he must have been *born* a marine. My older brother used to call him 'Testostosaurus rex.'

"Anyway, it was toward the end of the party; all the girls had left by now. I guess my friend's dad decided we needed to have 'boy time.' So everyone started playing football and his dad called this play. I wasn't paying attention—I was probably looking at some grasshopper or something, for all I know—and then I realize the ball's coming to me. I caught it, but then I just panicked. I started to run, but ran the wrong way.

"Well, this guy's father just reamed me out from top to bottom. Right there, at his son's birthday party, and in front of all his son's friends. It was unbelievable. My first reaction was, 'Oh my God, I really messed up.' I was devastated. But then I had this second reaction. I started to think, 'This guy's an asshole. I may have screwed up, but I didn't screw up as much as he's screwing up right now.'"

It takes a certain type of child to endure a humiliation like that and not come out of the experience a smaller human being. I considered Bill's ability to depersonalize the reaming-out at such a young age, and to see it as "the other guy's problem," to be pretty extraordinary. I asked him what he thought made him different back then from other eleven-year-old boys, most of whom would be crushed by this kind of incident.

Bill took a few moments to collect his thoughts before answering. "I think it comes down to having the ability to size up a scene from within your own perspective, and draw on your intrinsic self-worth as a way of shielding yourself from what the other person is saying. I wouldn't let Mike's dad define me as a loser. I had my own perspective on what had happened, one in which I wasn't a loser. I had crossed eyes as a kid, which gave me really bad depth perception. And I got disoriented a lot, in terms of right, left, up, down. I was just glad I caught the ball!" Bill smiled before looking away, and then turned back toward me again. His face was somber. "But it wasn't without its negative effects. You know, I tend now to be shy about taking on new experiences, and who knows, I might have been shy anyway. But I do know that whenever it's time to make any kind of 'big play,' I always doubt my ability to deliver. 'Put me in the outfield!' That's my motto. Don't give me a job too big or too important. I back away from that rather than set myself up for another Testostosaurus rex incident. I don't ever want to be there again—making the catch and then running entirely the wrong way."

Bill made it because he had a strong internal reference point to hold on to when others told him he was less than who he knew himself to be. His easygoing temperament and flexible personality style were huge factors as well. I've noticed that boys who survive being teased or marginalized tend to focus on what they do well, and don't take the bullies' messages to heart. They learn to entertain themselves, or find kids with shared interests. They also learn to seek out the company of grown-ups, or make friends with an extended relative or other adult who thinks they're just terrific and makes sure to keep telling them so.

Michael, twelve, was not an easygoing kid, nor was he particularly flexible. But he had something else working for him—a somewhat remote, albeit stout, personality that allowed him, like Bill, to avoid overpersonalizing what would otherwise have been insulting, derogatory remarks from different classmates over the years. Michael had a history of attention problems and a total disinterest in sports. During one of his ADD medication check-ups, Michael's doctor, a developmental pediatrician who happened to be quite sensitive to the issues surrounding nonathletic boys and sports, asked Michael about his friendships. "Most of my friends are into sports and I'm not," the boy had answered matter-of-factly, "but they make time for me." Michael didn't appear to resent the fact that his friends really liked sports and spent a lot of time playing them, nor did he appear to feel that only by playing sports would he be able to keep his friends. He had struck a nice balance where he felt worthy of friends, but not entitled to them.

Another boy, however, might have resented the sports, pressing his friends for more time in an attempt to prove to himself just how important his friendship was to them, and losing everything in the process. There are some boys who, in an urgent and desperate search for affirmation, find themselves standing alone in the end because they didn't understand that it's human nature to resent feeling beholden to someone who lays claim to your time or person without your consent.

Determination and pride were what Henry Dunow, author of *The Way Home: Scenes from a Season, Lessons from a Lifetime,* called on when it came time to shake off the homesickness that blindsided him at summer camp and transform himself into the athlete he'd never wanted or needed to become at home. Brought up in New York City by learned, intellectual parents who held sports in considerable disdain, Dunow had had, up until that point, very limited exposure to athletics. Soon after arriving at camp, though, Dunow saw the writing on the cabin walls. "In real life," he wrote, "you might be a violin prodigy, or a math genius, or just a happy, well-liked kid; here, if you were not an athlete, you were a worthless, second-class citizen." He summed up his experience in this way: "Overnight, I had gone from being a normal, popular kid . . . to a complete outcast . . . all because I couldn't field a grounder, dribble a basketball, or walk with an athlete's swagger. It was my first introduction to the brutal hierarchies of jock culture, and the point was made loud and clear: life was good for the kids who could play ball."

But Dunow decided he wasn't going to let himself be beaten by this cruel caste system; he would instead refashion himself into an . . . *athlete*. And so, over the course of his five seasons at summer camp, short, chubby Henry practiced doggedly, managing to rise above his mama's-boy roots and Yiddish-writer father heritage to become a scrappy little ballplayer upon whom the other boys had bestowed a new name—Hank.

Breaking

Fourteen-year-old Brandon tried faking it and it backfired on him big-time. Wearing oversize basketball jerseys, a Detroit Tigers hat off to the side, and a whole lot of five-and-dime-store bling, this skinny eighth grader who'd never played a game of basketball or baseball outside of phys ed class tried to pass himself off as something he was not. The boys he modeled himself after had both the muscular clout and personal swagger to pull this look off. But Brandon's ghetto look and brash humor convinced no one, and served only to highlight how out-of-sync he was with his peers. The reactions from the other kids ranged from bemused tolerance to outright disdain. Watching Brandon mingle with kids on the school grounds was painful, like watching a train whose conductor doesn't know that the bridge down the road is out.

By the time his parents brought him in for therapy, Brandon was an anxious wreck. He had stopped going to school following a weeklong series of panic attacks he'd had in the school hallway. He had stopped contacting the two or three boys who would occasionally hang out with him. There were few texts being traded on his cell phone. The only thing Brandon found himself able to do without either becoming anxious, or worrying about becoming anxious, was to immerse himself in video games and listen to his iPod. This poor kid tried so hard to be noticed that he became a caricature of ghetto cool. He had needed someone to tell him that the only thing worse than being a kid who doesn't fit in is being a kid who doesn't fit in and pretends not to know.

Brandon's parents, however, believed their son lacked only confidence, and because of this avoided saying anything that would have caused him to feel scrutinized. They never mentioned to him that he might have been dressed inappropriately, or that some of his jokes weren't all that funny. This was unfortunate, because what Brandon really needed was a caring family member or friend willing to help him recognize those times when his affections or humor weren't cutting it. So far, the only people telling him he wasn't funny or cool were the kids who avoided him because of it. And when they did tell him, they weren't very kind about it.

Parents whose children are anxious or insecure often try to protect them from even the child's own faculty of critical self-awareness. This rarely works out in the child's favor. What winds up happening is that these kids are allowed to remain oblivious to how trying some of their personal or social habits are for others to deal with. Of course this leaves it to those others—exasperated teachers, coaches, friends, relatives, and eventually roommates or partners—to tell them to tone it down or knock it off.

"The other day Nick asked me why he doesn't have a best friend." His mother, Ellen, was talking about her eleven-year-old son, whom she described as very intelligent, but also very bossy. She thought he tried to compensate for his lack of athletic ability by being smarter than everyone else. But instead of being smart in a way that other kids could like or respect, Nick chose to be smart by always insisting that he was right.

"I see him doing this and I want to stop him because I know it turns kids off to him," Ellen explained. "He's the same way at home, too. Every once in a while I try to say something about it, but he just gets really defensive, so I drop it. Nick's dad blames the lack of friends on the fact that Nick doesn't play a lot of sports, but I don't think that's it. Nick's always been able to find friends. He just doesn't keep them."

I told Ellen that I thought Nick could use an advocate, someone who would empathize with his feelings of insecurity while at the same time hold him a little more accountable for how those feelings drove his interactions with other people. Over time, the advocate would consistently, sensitively, and unapologetically help Nick understand that, no matter how urgently he needed to feel accepted, insisting all the time on being right wouldn't make other kids think he was smart. It would only make them think he wasn't so much fun to play with. And the best candidates to be advocates? In most cases, a child's parents.

"But I'd worry about hurting his self-esteem if I said something like that," Ellen replied. "He already feels down on himself for not being a 'sporty' kind of kid. I'd hate to make him feel worse."

Ellen needed to understand that talking with Nick about how he interacted socially didn't have to make him feel bad. It might make him feel a little self-conscious, but when handled kindheartedly, those types of conversations can leave children feeling hopeful about improving how they get along with others, if only by recognizing that they themselves are an integral part of making it better.

Kids like Nick need adults to (selectively and discreetly) give them this kind of feedback. Left on their own to figure things out, they're at risk for feeling at the mercy of social forces in which they play a role, but don't see or understand. That's a formula for becoming an angry, touchy, or defensive kid, one for whom it becomes even harder to see any personal contribution to the problem, and easier to instead blame everyone else.

Brandon was a crash-and-burn victim. He was so far out there by the time his parents recognized he was in trouble, and not going to mature out of it, that he needed a lot of time and therapy to rebuild his confidence and his real self. There are a lot of nonathletic boys who don't break like that, and whose experiences of being teased or excluded make a significant, but subtler, imprint on their personality and adjustment to adulthood. The following are some of the adaptations you'll see in these boys.

Withdrawal from activities

Nonathletic or insecure boys who've been stung by bad public sports experiences don't want to risk a repeat performance. So they stop doing things with other kids—unless they're very good at them. And they stop trying new things, because they're not good at them yet. Their worlds shrink as they live within, and remain defined by, the circumscribed range of activities in which they feel competent.

If you know a boy like this . . .

Sit down next to him one day and, when there's an easy, quiet moment, tell him you notice he doesn't seem to like trying new things anymore. If you remember or know of a time when he tried something new (sports-related or not) and was left feeling self-conscious or embarrassed afterward, let him know that you can appreciate how awkward it must have been for him, and how sometimes experiences like that make people not want to try new things. If you can, describe a situation in which that happened to you, and how you recovered.

What if you had a situation like that and didn't recover? *Tell him about that.* If you didn't recover, and if you still avoid new things for fear of looking dumb or out of the loop, *then tell him.* Kids need to hear more from us about the times we struggled socially or personally. Often, adults talk about where they've been successful in life, hoping that it will motivate their child to push through troubling or challenging situations. Sometimes, though, this can just wind up feeling like more pressure. Kids can also get a lot out of knowing that we really do understand how they feel when things don't go well, and that we understand why they make the choices they do, even if we don't agree with those choices. We connect most deeply through our humanity, not necessarily through our accomplishments.

Adopting the outcome as what they had wanted all along anyway

Some kids protect the image they have of themselves as being in control by making it seem as though things in their lives are going along exactly as planned. For example, seven-year-old Luke tried hard to convince me that he liked playing by himself. He wouldn't have wanted to play with anyone, he told me, "even if there were, like, a thousand kids here and they all were playing Pokémon . . ." Kids don't have a lock on this; adults do it, too: "There's no way I would ever have taken that job," a prospective hire says, after messing up her interview. "It wasn't at all how they described it." Most people like to feel as if they are the ones doing the choosing.

If you know a boy like this . . .

Parents of boys like Luke often just let remarks such as the one he made go. But what if they were to sit down next to him, pick up a few of those Pokémon cards, and say something like this: *I know you love to play with these cards, and you do a nice job of finding ways to play with them when you're by yourself. You say you like it better that way—and I believe that's true sometimes. But I also know that making friends is hard for you, and I wonder if you say you'd rather play by yourself even if there were a thousand kids here because it's easier to say that than to say you sometimes wish you had more friends.*

Maybe Luke would shake his head no or shrug his shoulders yes or do nothing at all, any of which is just fine. It's fine because the purpose is not to "get" him to admit that he really wants friends when he says he doesn't. The purpose in moments like this is only to make the unspoken spoken, unthreateningly, by a trusted adult in that child's life. Once it's out and on the table like that, it can be referenced or brought up again more easily in the future as you discover ways to help him deal with his disillusionment or disappointment about having few friends, or what might be feelings of shame surrounding the issue. It's also a good idea to speak to other parents and educators in the community who might know about special events going on related to your son's interests. Some libraries, for example, have Pokémon nights, where children come with their cards and play. If you have a good idea for a shared-interest play group, approach your local library or Y and see if they'd be willing to host it.

Defensive clowning

Some boys try to cope with their sense of isolation by becoming class cutups. They sacrifice their good standing with adults for the few moments of camaraderie they mistakenly read into the laughter their clowning evokes from other kids. The thinking, though rarely conscious, goes like this: *If I'm destined anyway to be the brunt of jokes, better that it seems as if I am the one pulling the strings. I will make them laugh at the things I decide are going to be funny, rather than be a sitting duck for someone else's prank—even if, in the end, it comes at my own expense.* To the casual observer, it looks as if the child is in control of it all, and having a good time. To the more astute observer, he looks miserable and demeaned.

Self-deprecating humor is what this same thing looks like in older boys and men, in essence, the class-clown upgrade.

If you know a boy like this . . .

It's tough convincing anyone that he's not as funny as he thinks he is. Rather than trying to "get" your son or this boy to see what he can't let himself see, try to have him talk about what he thinks his sense of humor is like, how he comes up with his jokes or gags, how he decides which ones are good and which ones aren't, and how he decides when to say or do them. Has he ever had a joke bomb, where nobody laughed? Tell him about a time when that happened to you, normalizing the experience, and making it a little easier for him to think about the times his attempts at humor have failed.

As a part of that conversation or even a separate one, consider telling your son that you sometimes worry he tries too hard to be funny and popular with the other kids in his grade. Then talk with him about the ways in which wanting something so much can make people do things they probably shouldn't do, like doing something that might get them in trouble just because some kids might think it's cool, or telling a joke that's inappropriate because it might impress a certain group of kids. This is also a great time to tell your son about times when you did something wrong or inappropriate or embarrassing in an attempt to fit in, or how you managed to stop yourself the times you were tempted to do something like that, but refrained. Then, at some point, let him know that you wonder if some of the times he gets in trouble at school for goofing off in class, or comes home from school mad because the other kids were teasing him, are times when he was trying to be funny or to impress some of the popular kids but it didn't go so well. Ask him if he'd like your help in figuring out what things are really funny and what things are not as funny as they might appear at first. Help him understand that stuff that seems so funny to think about can turn out all weird when you actually do it, and that's why everyone needs to be really careful if they're thinking of doing something that might get them in trouble or hurt someone's feelings.

Boys who act out this way in class sometimes don't recognize any positive ways they have at their disposal to get the attention of their peers. It's hard to get them to jump ship right off the bat, from being class cutups to indulging more of their pro-social traits or skills, not only because they lack confidence in them but also because those traits or skills might not carry any of the coolness factor thought to be associated with making the other kids laugh. Also, talking too much to kids about all the "positive" things they can do can sound patronizing, and turn some of these boys off altogether to anything you have to say about the subject. Anytime you find yourself "cheerleading" your son into showing or embracing his better self, stop, and come back to the issue another time with a fresh idea. When you're trying to get someone to go in the direction he's resisting, you almost always will get a better outcome by approaching the problem from the same side of the fence than by trying to pull him over the rail to your side, raw strength notwithstanding.

Overcompensating by Showing Off How Smart They Are

Boys who need an ego boost will sometimes overcompensate for what they don't have with something they do have—money, intelligence, a disarming amount of knowledge about a popular topic. I've had several boys come through my practice who, having been rejected for their nonathleticism, tried to recover their lost confidence by parading their intellect around for everyone to notice. Unfortunately, most of the time what people notice the most is that the boy is rather immodest or not very diverse or somewhat self-absorbed. Other kids might find him annoying, and alienate him further. Boys like this need help in understanding that being intelligent is terrific and potentially admirable, but only if it's part of a "bigger package." That package needs to include such things as knowing the difference between being proud and being conceited and knowing how to relate to others without having to play the smart card, among other skills. Left unguided, boys who do this sometimes can count among their real friends only older kids and adults.

If you know a boy like this . . .

Let him know that you notice and respect his smarts and like that he's proud of them himself. Then talk with him about what it's like to get to know someone, only to discover afterward that he can do this or that really well, and how much more impressive that is than finding out how good somebody is at something because that person keeps telling you so.

It's also a good opportunity for talking about grace and humility, and the importance of considering the impact of your actions and choices on the people around you. I often think many parents wait too long before introducing conversations about these things, or try to do it under the general heading of "Etiquette" (Be polite. Don't brag. Say you're sorry)—a rather unappealing invitation to discourse. Distilled down to platitudes, civic lessons about being a good person evoke very little of the interest in humanitarianism that more nuanced, candid discussions can bring about.

On the other hand, for families in which "deep" conversations are an anomaly, a little bit of chatter about overall good citizenship is usually better than a lot. Quick dips (e.g., *I think you really need to be more careful about how you say those things. It seems as if you're trying to sound like you're just giving information when you're really wanting to make a point . . .*) and "drive-bys" (e.g., *Sometimes I wish these things [e.g., being gracious, being considerate] were more important to you than it seems they are . . .*) allow you to get in with your point and get out before your kids know to brace against you. When kids realize that a parent isn't going to go on and on about something, they're less likely to be distracted from the message by their attempts to find a way out of the conversation.

Acting Too Mature for Their Age

Boys who feel marginalized by their peer group sometimes gravitate toward adults as safe havens and comfortable outlets for their social needs. The risk here, in addition to drifting further away from the peer group and developing affectations of being older than one's real age, is of commandeering the sympathy of these adults in ways that enable those behaviors further, in part by affirming the definition of the situation as "all the *other* kids' fault."

Hunter was a nine-year-old boy who had collected a cadre of relatives ready to pounce on the next kid who dared to take down their favorite nephew/grandson. They couldn't understand how such a mature and thoughtful child could evoke such animosity from other children. What they didn't see was the way in which Hunter's approach to relating to his peers—from a position of having matured beyond stupid jokes and verboten words and grossing out your friends—didn't play well in the fourth grade. Boys were supposed to like those things, but infinitely worse than not liking them was acting as if the other boys shouldn't like them either. *That's* what got Hunter picked on by the kids at school.

A sharp relative would have noticed that Hunter's response of burrowing more and more deeply into his self-righteousness would only make it harder for him to connect to his classmates. Besides, no matter how "correct" Hunter's perspective on the situation was, there would be no way for his relatives to constructively intervene on his behalf. Their influence stretched only as far as Hunter himself, the real agent of change in this scenario. Hunter needed someone to kindly, gently, and empathically tell him that, while they appreciated how important it had become to him that he appear mature for his age—and that he'd done a good job of it, too—he also needed to respect the fact that nobody really likes being told they're not grown up enough, especially by someone of their same age. Hunter also needed someone to model the joy that people of any age can experience when they let themselves be silly and play. It seemed that somewhere along the line, Hunter, like many other pseudo-mature kids, had thrown that baby out with the bathwater.

Kids' favorite adults have several things in common. For the most part, they're tolerant of differences in people and take an interest in lives other than their own. They keep their not-so-nice opinions of you to themselves. They aren't looking to mix it up with people who are slower or smaller or less popular than they are. They are safe to be around and sometimes say things that make you feel better.

One of the things adults say to children who seem especially mature for their age is that they'll make a great adult someday. They say it because they want the child to know that some of the personal qualities they see in him or her are things that are appreciated much more by adults than by kids. It's a promissory note of sorts, meant to give a child hope that there will be a time when he is recognized by his peer group. But if everyone mentions this brighter future only in a Pollyanna sort of way, and shies away from talking to the child about the difficult present—maybe because they don't want to "remind" him of his problems—the child may in turn feel a need to remind *them* of his problems so that they remain aware that until that future arrives, his everyday experience is anything but cheery.

THE LAST BOYS PICKED

If you know a boy like this . . .

See if you can engage him in a conversation about the relationships he has with different people—kids, adults, older adults.
Tell him you are aware that he seems to feel most comfortable
around adults, and that a lot of kids feel that way, especially if
they don't fit in perfectly with their classmates at school or worry
about being teased or left out.

Let him know that adults can be wonderful friends for kids,
but they can't be a kid's only friends. Share with him your observation that he tries to act real grown up a lot of the time, and that
while it probably is fine when he's with his grown-up friends, it
won't help him make friends with the kids his own age. You
might be tempted to tell him that it's because the kids his age are
too immature, but you shouldn't. For one thing, it's not true. The
disconnect between the boy you're talking with and his peers has
to do with the boy's behavior, not the peers', and he'll know that,
and realize you were willing to sacrifice the truth in order to
protect his feelings. The result is that you lose credibility and he
loses faith that you will always and under any conditions be
truthful with him. Second, it displaces the responsibility for
the problem onto the wrong person—the boy's peers, who are
just being typical kids. As a result, the boy isn't being encouraged
to gain perspective on himself as a good kid who has difficulty
feeling at home with kids his age. He's like everyone else whose
insecurities cause them to lose their real selves in the self they
think will impress others or is the one others want to see from

them. And before they know it, they don't remember anymore who their real self is.

The Importance to Kids of Saving Face

I'd been after Jake since the beginning of the school year to pick one of the after-school clubs to join. He was spending too much of his free time on the computer, and had too few other activities that he really enjoyed. It was early November, and there was still no club.

Soon afterward, though, Jake came home and announced that he was going to try out for the wrestling team. He was excited. I was excited, too, as were his dad and brothers. Jake tried out, made the team, and came home from school a couple of days later carrying a wrestling helmet and a pair of wrestling shoes. He put the helmet on for us and lightly batted his brothers around their ears.

The first day at practice went well. Walking through the front door, Jake spotted me and held his forefinger to his lips. I obliged his request for silence and thirty seconds later found out that I had become an accomplice to the ambush of Austin, who lay pinned on the family room floor. It was all good.

It was all good, that is, until the next day, when Jake came home from practice in a withdrawn, quiet mood. He spent almost the entire evening doing homework upstairs in his room.

The next day, Jake told me that he was quitting the wrestling team. I asked him why, and he evaded the question. I asked him again and he became defensive. I pressed for more. Finally he looked up at me, exasperated, and said, "What do you want me to say, Mom? That I got the crap beat out of me by three different kids?" I said, "Yes, I do, so I can know what's going on," but it felt thin and irrelevant, his dignity having handily eclipsed my empathy.

Thinking about it later, I felt bad for pressing Jake as I had and recognized the moment as a common one for parents torn between their wish or need to know what is upsetting their children and their desire to not make them feel worse about whatever is going on by talking about it. Maybe, if I had it to do over again, I'd say something to Jake about that instead—the dilemma I felt I was in—and then see where he took the conversation, if anywhere. Space and time and privacy are what Jake needed then, not questions about "what happened." I wanted to know what happened, but didn't really *need* to know right then. The more important need in that moment was his. When "empathic" responding has more to do with what the responder wants than with what the other person needs, it ceases to be truly empathic.

I recently sat with a fifteen-year-old girl who was trying to figure out how she was going to tell her parents she wanted to stay enrolled at the charter school they made her transfer to several weeks earlier. "It's just that I made such a big deal about how

I wasn't going to stay after the first semester," Heidi said. "Ever since they first mentioned my going there, I've said I would hate it, that it wasn't the school for me. They told me they'd let me go back to my regular school in January if I still wanted to return." The conflict for Heidi was her feeling that if she admitted to her parents that she liked the school and wanted to stay, they would think they "won." "What would they be winning?" I asked. "They'd win the whole 'who was right' and 'who was wrong' thing . . ." she replied. "And I know exactly what would happen—I'll tell them and they'll look at each other with this stupid smile on their faces and be thinking, 'Oh, we knew she'd come around.' They'll use it as proof that"—and here she mocked her mother's voice—"*we know you better than you know yourself!*' Ugh, I almost want to go back to my old school just so they won't get that satisfaction."

Lucky for Heidi she had the inner resolve to stay committed to the school of her choice even though it would mean having to watch her parents do their touchdown dance and tell her they knew all along she'd see it their way. I don't know what parents think they are accomplishing when they make a point to say "I told you so!" All it does is offend the child, and reveal a lack of sensitivity regarding how often teenagers are asked (or made) to subjugate their burgeoning autonomy to the edicts of parents and teachers. By choosing not to claim their daughter's decision to stay at the charter school as their victory, and by emphasizing their excitement for her rather than her "enlightenment," Heidi's parents would be allowing her to save face instead of feeling as if she had "given in." In doing so, they would be demonstrating a tremendous amount of respect for her courage to acknowledge wanting something her parents also wanted for her, and would receive in return her appreciation and confidence in them to not exploit opportunities to show who's boss.

These same kinds of inner quandaries exist for younger kids, too. Kids who have to be right will, in the face of inarguable evidence, refuse to change their mind; for them, being right is better than being smart. Kids who have to be independent will reject a parent's great idea for the sole reason that it wasn't theirs. "Solving a problem doesn't count unless you solve it on your own," a sad, aloof, hungry-for-contact girl of thirteen years once confided in me. Similarly, some kids who have a hard time defining their areas of competency will bristle when offered advice, because accepting the help summons their feelings of shame and inadequacy more than it invigorates what's left of their jaded confidence. There are times when the best thing we can do is stop talking, and stop making suggestions, and realize that what our sons need most in certain moments is our silent appreciation of the indignities they suffer, of what it takes to navigate the day, and then, let them simply save face.

Helping the Child Who Gets Defensive

Children who are defensive are very effective at getting people to back off and leave them alone. They may give the impression of being too sensitive or delicate or anxious or sad to handle what the other person wants to say, and as a result, very little gets said at all.

But many of these kids don't really want to be left alone. They just want to have others relate to them in ways that don't hurt. They don't say that, so others get the wrong impression—that they're disinterested, impersonal, prickly. If you have a child like this, talking to him may be very difficult. It may also be sad, or frustrating, because there's so much you want to say, but the windows of opportunity are small and fleeting. Sometimes they shut down right on your fingers.

Pushing talks on kids who don't want them makes adults seem pushy and kids obstinate. If viewed through their respective intentions, probably neither is true. It's just that the parent feels it's urgent, and the child feels imposed upon. So maybe that's the place for a parent to start: *I want so badly to talk with you about XYZ but don't know how to without feeling as if I'm forcing a conversation on you.*

Years ago I took my boys bowling. We paid two dollars each for two-toned shoes with big, Art Deco–looking numerals on the back of them and relaxed in plastic benches made in 1950s colors. Austin, a lefty, did okay, having to bowl with his right arm because of a strained left shoulder. Casey, sixteen at the time, did very well, pulling off a strike or two and a bunch of spares. I was marginally competent—a few gutter balls, lots of scores in the six, seven, and eight range. And up until his last roll, where he struck gold with a slow-rolling but steady-down-the-lane strike, Jake struggled. Gutter balls. Two pins. Gutter balls. One pin.

His brothers tried to help him. "Use your whole arm to swing, Jake! You're kind of just dropping it." "Try looking at the pins, buddy, not at the floor!" "Hey, dude, let's find you a different ball!"

But Jake got defensive, and grew sullen at the advice and support of his brothers. It wasn't because he didn't think he needed it. He looked away and acted annoyed because he was embarrassed. I mean, how many times can you be the worst before you finally say, *I don't want your stupid advice because it won't help anyway.*

Years later I revisited with Jake the trip to the bowling alley.

"Do you remember that night a few years ago when you, me, Austin, and Casey all went bowling?"

"Yeah," he said, his eyes locking with mine as he wondered where this was headed.

"Remember you had a hard time scoring that night, and Austin and Casey kept trying to give you tips?"

"Yeah, I remember."

"Well—" I started, and then stopped abruptly. *What was my question? What did I want to know?* It was as if I'd suddenly gotten shy, until it hit me that I was choking (again, as with the wrestling) under the pressure and responsibility of preserving a child's pride while asking him to respond to questions about an event he had experienced as painful. Just another one of the many moments of unexpected discomposure in parenthood.

I soon realized that what I wanted to know was if Jake had been able to enjoy any part of the evening even though he struggled with the bowling itself. I wanted to know if he'd been able to recognize the benevolence in his brothers' attempts to help, even if they had triggered his irritation. And finally, I wanted to know if he had the emotional scope to acknowledge the efforts of people to help him even when it wasn't working, and the grace and generosity of spirit to let them know it.

"Well," I began anew, "did you mind that they were trying to help you out? I mean, was that okay, or would you have rather they said nothing?"

"Said nothing," Jake muttered.

"Oh," I said. "Well, even though you weren't able to really benefit at the time from what they were telling you, were you able to appreciate that they were trying to help?"

"Well, yeah, but I really didn't want to hear it right then."

"Why not?" I finally braved.

"Because I didn't want to admit that I wasn't as good as everyone else!"

Of course not, and I get that now. I felt bad for making Jake do a second tour of duty through that evening and (once again) saw how difficult it can be for kids to separate their level of play from the degree of fun they derive from doing it. Understandably, these boys who spend years getting picked last develop an acute sensitivity to being placed last anywhere, and in any company. They come to a bowling alley or skating rink or mini golf course with a different agenda than the other boys, who come to win, or at least to have fun. Boys like Jake come with the objective of avoiding humiliation or demoralization; it's a whole different mind-set. At the bowling alley that day, Jake didn't need advice as much as he needed our quiet appreciation for his being a good sport in going along with an afternoon plan decidedly *not* of his making. Casey, Austin, and I might have come away from it being ever-so-slightly better bowlers, but in retrospect, Jake came away a class act.

The Fire That Melts the Butter Hardens the Egg

Because of their innate psychological makeup, and/or the life circumstances from which they grew resilient, and/or the family system that raised and supported them, a great many boys respond to the challenges of gender-role expectations in adaptive rather than maladaptive ways. Some do it right off the bat, while others get there after taking a lap through some of the behaviors discussed in this chapter. Jack, for instance, computer software engineer and father of two, was able to identify one way in particular that being marginalized for his small size and lack of athletic ability ended up working in his favor: He developed a very clever sense of humor, which, in turn, made him quite popular in his middle school.

"I did come away from it all with some things I probably wouldn't ever have learned or developed," Jack said, referring to his elementary school years in which he spent a lot of time warding off bullies. "For instance, it definitely brought out more of my humor. I mean I have kind of a wry attitude toward it all now, but I remember thinking, 'I'll never be recognized for my athleticism but I sure as hell can make them laugh.' I saw being funny—not goofy funny but, like, witty funny—as my ticket out of having to walk around looking over my shoulder all the time. It's probably the only thing that can really draw respect from kids who otherwise would have nothing to do with you."

By capitalizing on his wit and humor, Jack had tapped into an unexpected source of power—cracking people up. Deborah Tannen, author of *You Just Don't Understand: Women and Men in Conversation*, notes how the ability to make somebody laugh is a huge feat of momentary power—and another way of negotiating social status. She points out that the linguist Wallace Chafe considered a person's spontaneous eruption into laughter to be a form of losing control, even if very brief. It's pleasurable for the laugher, but a real high for the comedian, a coup of sorts. No wonder stand-up comics persist in spite of daunting humiliation: When it's bad, it's awful, but when it's good, there's nothing like it.

Let's go back for a moment to boys who adapt constructively to the challenges they faced growing up; as men, some of them talk about how their social alienation pushed them into areas they wouldn't otherwise have chosen. Mostly this takes place in high school, where more outlets for creative and innovative expression materialize. "It spurred me on to do other things," recalled Doug, "like the school newspaper." Since it provided much more of a safe haven than the gym locker room could ever have been, it's not surprising that Doug gravitated to a club room where social currency was measured in terms of verbal fluency and a sociopolitical consciousness.

Other boys do share Doug's good fortune at having been able to isolate a measure of personal or emotional growth that came from unfortunate social experiences. Carl, as a thirteen- and fourteen-year-old boy, experienced a swelling sense of compassion for the kids who, through no fault of their own, were put in situations where they'd have to go along with institutionalized discrimination they didn't personally support. "The weird thing was," he said, "after a while I started feeling sorrier for the captain picking the team than I did for myself. Because there was always that moment when there'd just be me and another kid left and here's this guy who's supposed to pick one and not the other and I'd think, 'I don't know who's worse off—that guy, or me?' I know that some of them actually felt sorry for me and would have picked me but felt they couldn't, because if they had, the guys on their team would have gotten mad at them. As far as I'm concerned, that old 'line the boys up and pick 'em one at a time' method for putting together a team is barbaric. I have no idea how a gym teacher, or *any* adult, could watch that go down and not call an immediate halt to it." Carl adds, "I mean, really, *what was anybody thinking . . . ?*"

Good question.

CHAPTER FIVE

The Dangers of Romanticized Masculinity

Years ago I knew a mother who had eight kids, the last six of whom were boys. The father was deceased, so the mom counted on the older two girls and a few aging relatives to help maintain the household and care for the boys. The brothers were energetic, scrappy kids, the kind who manage to make do with less and never come up short. Outside of the home, they were likable and polite, but inside the home they fed off each other's impish troublemaking and made watching over them nothing short of a Herculean task.

I remember this family because, despite the mother's spoken expectations that all of the children pitch in around the home, she remained unusually accepting of her sons' casual avoidance of their chores and disregard for limits. "I don't know what it is with boys and their socks . . ." she'd say, amusedly. Or, "I don't know what it is with boys and going to bed. Seems no matter how many times I tell them to start settling down, they just can't ever get enough of their horsing around . . ." And you'd just know that she had spent the evening before picking up stray socks and nipping at her sons' heels like a border collie, herding them through their showers and into their beds and probably thinking to herself something along the lines of, *They sure run me ragged, these boys, but I guess that's boys for you.*

Thinking of that mom always reminds me of another, who'd come to see me for help with her one seventeen-year-old son. The son, Andre, spent most of their first appointment trying to convince both his mom and me that his near-daily habit of smoking pot had no bearing on his slumping grades or darkening mood. Andre's mother was trying to buy it, but—thankfully—couldn't get over the hump; I think she'd been hoping to be persuaded. That way, she wouldn't have had to play the heavy and risk messing up their carefully engineered relationship—the one in which Andre allowed his mother to believe that the two of them shared a very close bond so long as she didn't interfere too much with his life.

> Our culture seems to expect its teens to be a little coltish and unruly. You see this in parents' tolerance for their kids' "typical teenage behavior." Teenagers can do better, and they know it, but why wouldn't they capitalize on this romanticized view of adolescence? Kids can take advantage of the parents' anxiety over scholastic achievement, their desire to avoid conflict, and their wish to see their children be happy and successful, and get them to shoulder the responsibility for everything from making sure assignments are in on time to making sure there is a pressed shirt for their seventeen-year-old's job interview.
>
> Janet

Andre had a strikingly sophisticated sense of humor that lent the relationship between him and his mother a peerlike quality. Plus, in the absence of Andre's dad, who had left the family a long time before and surfaced briefly only every few years, Andre's mother seemed to have ever so subtly drafted her son into the role of "man" around the house, to which he offered no objection. Against such a backdrop, Andre's mother was finding it very hard to separate her role as parent from the camaraderie they'd established over the years.

In each of these cases, all the boys were being given tremendous latitude in both their behavior and their autonomy, neither of which any one of them was handling well. The first mother's potential diligence had given way to her view of boys as lovable scamps, their transgressions a burden she'd willingly bear for the privilege of raising her own half dozen of them. The second mother was oblivious to the dangers being courted by her son's smoking and glib manipulations. Seeing them would have meant either having to act on her suppositions, or realizing that her wish to avoid conflict with her son and maintain their dynamic was immobilizing her as a parent. Distracted by their adoration for their sons and blinded by the boys' roguish charm, both moms had managed, unfortunately, to lose sight of the difference between boys, and boys who are behaving badly.

This is no small oversight, Christina Hoff Sommers, author of *The War Against Boys: How Misguided Feminism Is Harming Our Young Men*, reminds us; and the ante is even higher when the behavior we're talking about is really bad, i.e., physical aggression, duplicity, violations of personal rights. Because in failing to see the difference between boys, and boys who are behaving badly, we leave room for bad behavior to be seen as just another facet of masculinity instead of as a function of poor mental health, family dysfunction, or, increasingly, poor socialization.

Sommers acknowledges up front that males are naturally more physically aggressive than females. Studies across different cultures tell us these differences show from the time children begin to play together as toddlers. However, while males by nature are more aggressive than females, *most are not aggressive*

EXPECTING MORE FROM BOYS . . .

Our culture encourages us to foolishly set the bar lower for boys than for girls when it comes to decent behavior and moral sensibilities. I do believe that it's harder for young boys than it is for young girls to keep aggressive or competitive impulses in check, but it shouldn't mean we don't ask them to do it. By affording boys an exaggerated growth curve for controlling aggression, tolerating frustration, or being responsible for how their choices impact others, we actually wind up patronizing them and, in a sense, defining them as the "less civilized" gender. And then we're surprised when they don't quickly transition into the mature, responsible young men we expect them to be just a few years later, at eighteen or twenty-one.

inappropriately. And when they are, it's not because they're boys, but because they're boys who often have been inadequately socialized.

I think it's fair to say that, taken as a group, boys will always demonstrate more over-the-top, risk-taking, trash-talking, envelope-pushing behavior than will girls, partly because they're wired that way and partly because our culture encourages it. Nevertheless, it seems important that parents, educators, mentors, and others whose lives intertwine with children learn to recognize the point where boyish antics slip down the slope and become *unsociable* antics. That's how we can begin reversing the tendency of many (mainly females) who, viewing "boyhood" through rose-colored glasses, choose not to hold boys and men accountable for pulling the plug on behavior that is unbecoming, if not downright unpleasant. There is really nothing romantic about boys who are flippant about having to carry their weight in relationships, or who think the rules of society or their community or their own family don't apply to them. There's nothing romantic about boys who, in the name of joking around, find entertainment in making other people feel self-conscious or embarrassed. It's all so distasteful and ugly, and we should be stopping it.

Admittedly, it can be hard to know exactly where to draw the line between what's cute or charming, and what's offensive or exploitive. The romantic veil that gets placed over the sketchy behavior of so many boys masks a lot of inappropriate conduct. Shrewd guys take advantage of this all the time, oscillating between charismatic confidence and a waggish charm for the audience of females they hope to disarm, and then seduce. This

RESISTING THE INCLINATION TO WHITEWASH "BAD-BOY" BEHAVIOR

Parents enamored with their son's cleverness or list of accomplishments sometimes don't see their more unpleasant, arrogant, or immature behavior. Over time, these boys learn to take advantage of their ability to distract parents with their winsome personalities, and use it to gain privileges and favors and, commonly, a level of independence for which they really aren't ready.

Use the following questions to help differentiate between "boyish" behavior and bad behavior:

1. Would you look at the behavior differently if he were a she?
2. Do you feel as if you were charmed out of responding the way you had wanted to respond?
3. Do the behaviors bother you, even though they may amuse other people?
4. Do the behaviors make your son appear immature?
5. Do your son's "antics" embarrass you? Are they annoying to other kids or coming at someone's expense?
6. Do you ever notice adults getting offended?

bad-boy-as-sexy-boy creates problems not only for the girls who end up taking these boys at face value, but for the "good" boys too, who, by comparison, come off as lacking in mystery or menace, and are ultimately desexualized.

The act of romanticizing always blurs the picture; that way we get to see only what we want to see. In its wake, everything becomes more manageable. There's much less work when you don't have to get to know every person from scratch. But when a whole population of males is romanticized, and the gender is distilled down to a handful of pop-culture descriptors, then this becomes the human conglomerate that individuals relate to, instead of the one standing before them.

Only when we're willing to give up control over the perceptions we develop of other people can we allow them to be seen for who they are. That means letting each boy be different—roguish, reticent, virtuous, effervescent, or emboldened beyond belief—and waiting long enough for him to tell us who he is before deciding that for him. They are, as we say, who they are. We lose the romantic vision, approaching guys this way. But with the forfeiture we gain clarity and a more honest experience of the other person. It's by far the better deal.

Normalizing Bad-Boy Behavior

I agree with Christina Sommers when she defines bullying as a moral problem, not a behavioral one. I say that because, in the microcosm of a bully's assault on another child, we can see almost the entire set of principles upon which his interactions with others rest. As well, he shows us his holes: a lack of empathy, a belief in the primacy of might, what may be his desperate need for control, and an unwillingness to yield to anyone seen as inferior. This is so much bigger than just behavior, and because of that, the solution requires a different plan of attack and different remedial strategies than what might be put together for kids who don't complete their homework assignments or come home before curfew.

Whether it's innate, or acquired from their respective environments, or due to a lack of socialization, or some mix of these, boys have a long history of doing odd or mischievous things that amuse grown-ups and make them think, *Well, there's a boy for you!* Norman Rockwell understood this very well, and made a good living from it. It's no wonder we've wound up with boys who, almost by definition, *have* to drink out of milk cartons, carry worms in their pockets, and court trouble. It even seems that a lot of adults believe the masculine spirit is actually *imperiled* when boys are socialized at too early an age. Maybe that's why so many of them see their sons' yelling, restlessness, and impulsivity as part of being a boy, rather than as behaviors to be tempered. More than a few unruly five-, six-, and seven-year-old boys have been brought through my practice by parents with a seeming sense of pride in having a little ruffian of a kid: *I make "real" boys,* their shared grins project, oblivious to how this feeds their son's future character.

Consider an example offered up by psychologist Anthony Rao and Michelle Seaton in their book *The Way of Boys: Raising Healthy Boys in a Challenging and Complex World*, in which a young boy's intense need to be top dog was just steamrolling over his kid sister's due share of shoddy rights. The boy was constantly claiming—and getting, from his overaccommodating (as I see it) parents—the favored dinner plates or better booster seat, or orchestrating contests that his little sister stood no chance of winning ("First one to the front door . . ."). Left at the mercy of her brother's bossy, domineering behavior, the despairing little sister would simply give up or cry. Rao was using this example to illustrate how parents often get too stressed out over their sons' meltdowns and attempts to control outcomes, and wind up micromanaging their behavior. Under the doctrine of "letting boys be boys," his advice for this particular boy's mother was to let the two children work it out between themselves and address it only when their behavior got out of control.

As far as I could tell, though, the situation was already out of control. Justified by the importance he placed on winning, this little boy was essentially being given permission to act aggressively toward his sister, even in the face of her obvious distress. That's not boy behavior; it's poor behavior. The boy learns nothing constructive from being allowed to indulge his wishes of making everything a competition and rigging the winnings. He learns instead that the responsibility for your actions is conditional upon what you want, how badly you want it, and how you feel. His sister, in turn, learns only to resent her bully brother, and question the credibility of her parents as adults who can discern unjust behavior from just, and respond accordingly. It seems, actually, a good example of how to condition boys to be unbearably boorish.

This is exactly how adolescence gets its undeserved reputation

DON'T LET YOUR BOYS STEP ON ANTS

It's one of those things that could seem like no big deal: A kid sees an ant crawling across the driveway, and rides his bike over it.

But it was an animal's *life*. And it was just snuffed out because . . . why? The boy doesn't like ants? Because he could do it? Because that's what boys do? They are all terrible reasons to take a life, and by not stepping in to stop it, we are inadvertently *endorsing a respect for life that is conditional upon power and control*—exactly the thing we're trying to get away from.

Things to Say to Boys About Ants and
Other Small Creatures:

Please don't do that anymore. I know that a lot of boys think of bugs as annoying, or as if their lives don't count, but I think it's cruel to destroy anything just because you don't want it around, or worse, because you can. I want you to grow up with a great respect for life in all its forms, and to never think of it as being your place to decide who gets to stay on this planet and who doesn't. Once you do, you've turned yourself into a bully.

Or, Hey, I know you're the type of kid who would never hurt any of your pets and would probably be willing to get in someone's face if you thought they were hurting their dog or something. That's why it bothers me to see you and your friends treat bugs as if they were there for you to play with. First of all, you assume they don't experience pain, or if you think they do, then why would you ever put a creature in that situation? And please don't say I'm making too big a deal over this, or that it was only a few ants, because to me it will never be a numbers thing. It's a "what kind of person do you want to be" thing—someone who gets their pleasure from taking advantage of and hurting others, or someone who takes a stand in this world against inflicting undeserved pain.

for "Sturm und Drang," a self-fulfilling prophecy disguised as developmental theory that lulls parents into complacency with their adolescents' moodiness or defiance. Adolescents really don't have to be all that moody or defiant, and they certainly do not have to be rude. We've come to believe *they're just wired that way,* but no, they go there because we let them.

Hands-Off Parenting: Oxymoron

Arguments against too much hands-on parenting have been around since at least the time of eighteenth-century Swiss philosopher Jean-Jacques Rousseau. He believed that all children were born noble and virtuous by nature; they got ruined only when people tried to socialize them. "Rousseauian romanticism" is what Christina Sommers calls the approach of parents and educators who naively celebrate the supposed innate goodness of kids while abandoning the responsibility to civilize them. Lou Marinoff, author of *Plato Not Prozac!: Applying Eternal Wisdom to Everyday Problems,* frankly labels Rousseau's philosophy of education "a recipe for disaster."

"I've often heard it said that girls are much more difficult to raise than boys. To bring up a healthy young man, a parent need only leave him to his own devices, and hope he turns out to be a productive member of society. Of course, the idea that boys somehow need less attention has backfired, and parents and educators are only now beginning to understand the adverse effects of not paying attention to our boys."

John Nikkah, with Leah Furman, *Our Boys Speak,* p xiii

Fast-forward two hundred years or so and you'll hear echoes of Rousseau in the child liberation movement that took place in the United States in the 1960s. John Leo, author of the 1999 article "Parent-Free Zone," wrote that "[a]s the civil rights movement broadened to include women and gays, children, too, were depicted as an oppressed minority in need of liberation." What developed was an ideology about child rearing and child development that highly valued autonomy over socialization.

In her book *Ready or Not: What Happens When We Treat Children as Small Adults,* Kay Hymowitz traces the problematic trickling of these ideas into mainstream parenting and education where they crystallized into a philosophy she calls "anticulturalism." Essentially, anticulturalism teaches that children should be left pretty much to develop on their own. Well, we know what happens when this utopian view of childhood meets the light of day: Wherever they can, schoolboys make jelly out of whichever poor kid came in last in the Thanksgiving Turkey Trot.

Nowhere is this debate over the true nature of boys better or so graphically depicted than in William Golding's novel *Lord of the Flies,* in which the alleged internal conflict between civilizing and barbarizing instincts is played out horrifically among a group of British schoolboys stranded on an island and left to fend for themselves without adult supervision. Golding's story casts ruthlessness as the victor over benevolence, underscoring his belief that when human beings follow rules and behave decently, it is because they were taught to do so.

Anticulturalism isn't the only mitigating force against hands-on parenting and consistent socialization. Scores of researchers, social scientists, and psychologists have been telling parents for years that it's not their fault their kids are on drugs (because it's in the genes) and it's not their fault their kids unmercifully impose their angry humor on the household (because it's in the hormones) and it's not their fault their kid is embarrassingly rude to them in public (because all teens need to test limits and push their parents' buttons).

This is the message Judith Rich Harris blasted forth with in 1998 with her book *The Nurture Assumption: Why Children Turn Out the Way They Do*. This popular book relieved parents of the burden of responsibility for reflecting on—and modifying—the influence they have on their children's psychological development by elevating the importance of nature over nurture. This is a slippery slope if there ever was one, not dissimilar to what happens when we allow masculinity itself to be blamed for the poor behavior of unsocialized boys.

Tucked away in a splendid little book called *The Good Citizen*, professor, author, and activist Dr. Cornel West wrote a chapter about the moral responsibilities of living in a democratic society. He sees our current society as having become increasingly decadent, with eroding systems of caretaking and spiritual cultivation. Nurturing today is difficult, says West, because we're bombarded by a market culture that revolves around buying, selling, promoting, and advertising. In that kind of social climate, it is hard for *nonmarket* values such as mercy, justice, care, service, solidarity, and fidelity to drive the larger choices that people end up making with regard to finding mates or selecting careers, child rearing, and the overall direction their lives will take.

Maybe that explains why people beef up their business or golf skills at rates far greater than they do any of the ones related to parenting. It reminds me of the time when my oldest son got his first job. Hired at a local convenience mart, Casey received more training on making sandwiches in his first two weeks than most adults get on parenting over the course of their entire lives. We all say that raising children is one of the most challenging jobs a mother or father will face. Why then is our society so complacent about this learn-as-you-go method of parenting that has served as the default model for as long as anyone can recall? And, given that for many parents it is also the most important job they'll ever have, and that the ramifications of good versus bad parenting on everyone are so many and so significant, it's stunning to me that on-the-job training remains, in our culture, the instructive model of choice.

The Difference Between Loving and Coddling

"He's tough, he's a boy. He can take it," says a father about his six-year-old son, who just got knocked flat on his face by an older brother testing out his brand-new bike. Sure he can take it. What choice does he have?

But "can" is a different experience from "should." Just because he *can* take it, does it mean he should have to? The argument in favor of this is that the boy grows a thicker skin and learns that he is seen as a kid who can handle himself. Whether this is something the boy likes, or finds comforting, may depend on the reaction he gets from others and quite likely his father in particular.

Feeling that you're tough and can take it isn't an unhandy feeling either; it's a good one to have in your back pocket when you want to stand your ground in the face of some challenge or threat. On the downside, the boy learns that his dad can be insensitive at times to what hurts him and what doesn't; worse perhaps is learning that his dad makes those determinations for him.

One argument against the "he's tough and can take it" school of hard knocks is that, well, *the kid is only six years old*. Has he really already outgrown his need to know that his parents have his back? Or is someone outgrowing this for him? Our sons will tell us loudly and clearly when we're not needed in the clubhouse anymore; we don't have to worry about missing our cue. One day, their appreciative acceptance of our ministrations is supplanted with the words *I'm fine, Mom*, and we're to understand from this that our days running over with blue freeze ice packs or Sponge-Bob first-aid kits are over.

But what about this: Why not use these twilight years of early childhood to train the next crew of attendants—that being the boys themselves? Meaning that a father, after observing his eight-year-old boy play in the park, makes a point of saying to him, *Hey dude, when you jumped off the slide, you kind of knocked into that kid over there, the one who's looking like he's trying not to cry. Why don't you go over and see if he's all right? Make sure he knows it was an accident.* Or that a mother, seeing her daughter get knocked around pretty hard in field-hockey practice, suggests to the girl's older brother that he discreetly check in on her. So that, ultimately, when a neighborhood game of Capture the Flag gets a

BE A PART OF DEBUNKING THE ROMANTICIZING OF BOYHOOD BY PUBLICLY RESISTING THE IDEA THAT BOYS ARE TOUGH AND DON'T NEED "CODDLING"

Let the saying *He's tough, he can take it* be our cue to chime in casually with a countering remark that communicates, *He probably could, but are we sure we want to make him?* Examples include:

- "These poor guys, we're so busy telling them how big and tough they are and for all we know they're thinking, *But I'm only five, Ma. I don't want to be so big and tough yet . . .*"

- "I don't know, sometimes I think as parents we get so worried we're going to coddle our sons that we go too far in the other direction, and maybe don't give them enough affection."

- "Sometimes I feel bad for little boys, actually. It's, like, there they are with skinned knees and a scuffed nose and probably wanting a little TLC, but they've been told, *Don't expect much in the way of sympathy because you're supposed to be tough now.* Sometimes I want to go over and just hug my kid and he's over there looking like he would love nothing more but neither one of us makes a move because we're 'not supposed to' want that. It's kind of crazy . . ."

little too physical, there will be children with the sensitivity and confidence and interpersonal skill sets to go over to the kid lying on the ground and ask him if he's okay, needs any ice, wants a hand up.

Our kids need roles in their lives other than student, friend, athlete, or member of the marching band, and some of them should be caregiving ones. Our society seems to have such fixed ideas about who gives to whom: Adults give and kids get. Children need to learn that they, too—of their own accord and quite effectively—can address the needs of another, and that this need not be experienced as burdensome. A lot of kids do this already through small but noble acts of gallantry that sometimes challenge the social status quo. These are kids with the confidence, or the conviction if nothing else, to assume the risk that these types of challenges can incur, e.g., alienating a peer group, offending or embarrassing an adult. Beth's eleven-year-old son, Ethan, did something like this in his fifth-grade phys ed class. Attending an American school in Abu Dhabi, Ethan spoke up upon hearing the teacher tell the boys to divide themselves into two teams. Aware that this would be disastrous to his one British friend, who was destined to be the last one left standing, Ethan politely suggested to the teacher that they simply count off instead—*one, two, one, two . . .*

A certain percentage of the population will always argue against teaching boys to be more empathic, believing that it puts them at risk for being too vulnerable, too "soft." To me, it sounds a lot like the same argument people raise against "loving children too much"—which I see more accurately as "setting limits too little." Talking about empathy (or compassion or love) in this way turns the whole thing into a zero-sum equation: To the degree that a boy develops a greater capacity for empathy, he loses a corresponding amount of stoicism /masculinity/competitiveness. Really? Why can't boys have a lot of both? Jeez, if we can't envision males who are empathic and masculine or strong, then *how the heck are we ever going to raise them?*

The Boy Code

Men and boys run a pretty tight club, one beauty of it being that all of their rules and codes of conduct are handed down without benefit of contracts or bylaws or training manuals or even note cards. Most guys probably couldn't even tell you where or when all that handing down takes place. It just does, in all those invisible moments and forgotten spaces in between people and places and events, places where boys learn without knowing they're being taught that you're supposed to do that instead of this, say this instead of that, never admit to you-know-what, and always do XYZ when some other boy does ABC. Of course the downside to this unobtrusive schooling is that all these rules and codes just keep getting handed down one generation after another, without benefit of revision or modernization, sticking everyone with masculine ideals more suitable for the Colosseum or the Wild West than for twenty-first-century living.

Look a little closer, and you'll see another fly in the ointment.

The club guidelines may help boys grow up to be guys, but some of the values they shape in boys and men are actually incongruent with values and personality traits often thought to be associated with men of good character. Take, for example, the four basic, stereotyped male ideals or models of behavior[1] that the author of *Real Boys: Rescuing Our Sons from the Myths of Boyhood*, William Pollack, describes as being at the heart of "Boy Code." The first one urges boys to remain stoic and independent at all times, masking any weaknesses or insecurities. This is the very opposite of the honesty and emotional accessibility that philosophers Aristotle and Plato had encouraged in their young charges. It's also contrary to the concept of transparency inherent in "Purity"—one of the knightly virtues, that ruling code of honor assembled by no less manly a source than the male elders of the High Middle Ages.

A second injunction of Boy Code endorses the thrill-seeking, risk-taking nature of boys, but ratchets it up some. Bravado and daredevilry and the wish to resolve all matters through physicality become the ideal, in contrast to a more knightly "Prudence," which counsels circumspection, among other things, and the self-restraint implied by its sibling virtue, "Temperance."

A third tells boys that real males pursue status, power, and dominance over others, while a fourth admonishes boys for expressing anything that could be mistaken for dependency, vulnerability, or empathy. Looking at it this way, a lot of what our boys learn about being men flies in the face of what we teach people about being good human beings—humility, mercy, benevolence, justice—suggesting, and rather ironically, too, that at least on some level, Boy Code and a virtuous, knight-worthy life do not make good bedfellows.

It's an amusing juxtaposition on paper; however, in real life, trying to balance these two contradictory honor calls is no laughing matter for boys. Moreover, who is teaching that second honor call? Has gender socialization become the more prominent process of acculturation for children, making kids and parents think more about raising true-to-type boys and girls than about raising good human beings?

CHAPTER SIX

Boys in Straitjackets

In our hurry-up-and-get-there society, girls are given a nice little grace period in childhood during which they can just be girls. No one implores them to "knock it off" when they cry or "act like a woman" when they become frightened. With some unfortunate exceptions, they are allowed to be children. By the time puberty and adolescence come, most girls are already well on their way to becoming young women and more than eager to shed their girlishness in favor of a more knowing, less naive female self. The process is natural and the timing organic; girls become women because they're ready, and not because they've been shamed out of being girls.

We generally respond more strongly and more negatively to precocious maturity in girls than in boys. It makes us uncomfortable, and some of the behaviors associated with it are unbecoming.

On the more benign side are the girls who righteously scold their peers for not being as grown up as they themselves have some- how managed to become, or who assume a protective, maternal role among their friends. Much scarier is the young girl who demonstrates her pseudo maturity through sexuality. Consider the surreal look of those miniature beauty queens in the film *Little Miss Sunshine,* who mimicked the demure posturing of movie stars decades their senior, and who wore makeup they needed a good ten years or so to grow into.

It's different for boys, though. They don't get as long a grace period during which they are recognized and treated as children— sensitive, vulnerable, innocent in their affections for others. They are "men in the making," ushered quickly through those phases of childhood toward more narrowly defined identities in which they will learn to tamp down their emotionality and obscure any personal transparency that might already have been showing. "Boys have the sensitivity routinely mocked and shamed and beaten out of them, and the treatment leaves scars for life," ob- serves Norah Vincent, who spent a year and a half disguised as a man, an experience she wrote about in her book *Self-Made Man: One Woman's Journey into Manhood and Back Again.* "Yet we women wonder why, as men, they do not respond to us with more feeling. Actually, we do more than that. We blame and disdain them for their heartlessness."

Vincent is right to point out the lousy deal guys are handed. As boys, they are brought up and socialized to check their feel- ings at the door—not the door leading in, but the one leading out, into public view. Look ahead a few years, and they're being admonished by móms or girlfriends who (surprise!) are now finding their sons and boyfriends too emotionally remote; these women had been hoping to see a little more emotional IQ peeking out from underneath their shirtsleeves and, in particular, signs of modern-day guy *sensitivity*. That is, of course, as long as they're not too obvious about it—unless they're gay, in which case it's okay. Guys who don't curb their emotionality just right earn unwelcomed comments such as, *Oh, my fiancé is such a girl—he cries every time we go to the movies.*

What a conundrum for guys who want simply to grow up and be emotionally genuine without worrying about how far they've strayed from the masculine "ideal," polarized preposterously from its feminine twin in the form of the über-macho man, a living parody of gender.

Of course, guys who aren't comfortable modeling themselves after the hunky he-man have the New Age man to consider instead. Caricature being ever the tagalong sibling of polarization, these two models of masculinity are often forced to square off with each other, or

> "In a country where a two-year-old girl who slips on Daddy's loafers is greeted with laughs, but a two-year-old-boy teetering on Mommy's heels sets off panic alarms, manliness is a sticky issue."
>
> Carrie Rickey, *Philadelphia Inquirer* movie critic, on *I Love You, Man*

are juxtaposed for effect, as in the tagline for Tripp Lanier's the New Man podcast "Beyond the Macho Jerk and the New Age Wimp." Comic exaggeration aside, our culture's modern New Age man is actually a pretty sensitive and compassionate guy, at ease with the prospect of talking about feelings. Most recently, he's taken to showing up in a bunch of rom-coms and "bro-mances," where he cares deeply for his best guy friends and is willing even to tell them so. Take *I Love You, Man,* the 2009 comedy starring Paul Rudd and Jason Segel as two guys be-friending each other. The movie, says *Philadelphia Inquirer* critic Carrie Rickey, "takes aim at a culture where any dude who does not measure up to the muscular, hoops-shooting, steak-eating, fantasy-football-drafting, poker-playing, beer-ad picture of guy-ness is immediately subject to whispers about his manhood."[1]

Of course, the danger, as Rickey points out, of identifying too closely with the New Age guy is the risk of being seen as unmas-culine, which is a second cousin to being a little too feminine, which is a second cousin to maybe being gay. Guys go to great lengths not only to appear masculine, but to not appear, in any way, feminine. And that means having to jettison, or at least keep from view, all those supposedly feminine traits like being empathetic and caring about your relationships. "As a male, I am insulted by the stereotype that I am expected to kill bugs or lift things or play sports because of my gender," remarked Tony, on his webpage "Gender: Getting Beyond the Differences," "the same way females should be expected to cook, clean the house, sew, or 'dress pretty' because of their gender. I'm totally unath-letic, as are many other males . . . Likewise, there are numerous females who have outstanding athletic abilities. But just because a male is unathletic doesn't mean he's 'gay.'"[2]

Of course not, but that doesn't stop people from making those kinds of assumptions; it's another way they try to keep their world more manageable: *If something's this, then it must also be that.* Or, its obverse: *If something's that, then it certainly can't be this.* It's a tidy, time-managed filing system that obviates the need to actually get to know people before they are "properly" classified.

This collective societal anxiety about homosexuality gets in the way of a lot of things, one being our ability to have conversations with each other about the biases others or we hold with regard to nonnormative gender behavior and sexuality. As a result, parents, educators, youth leaders, counselors, and kids all miss out on chances to deal more directly with prejudices that come out in an institution's or in a person's behavior or words and then are promptly denied. They lose out, too, on opportunities to chip away at the subtle equations of nonathleticism with hypomasculinity, and build a different quality of public dialogue.

The truth of the matter is that only a small percentage of nonathletic boys are gay. As I see it, the problem has less to do with "is he or isn't he" than with the matter of withheld thoughts and aborted conversations. Parental anxieties, in particular, about the sexuality of nonathletic boys keep some families on guard against saying the "wrong" things, creating a layer of reserve or self-consciousness in everyone. In addition, it prevents parents from talking candidly with their sons (*You used to get so upset whenever the kids at school would call you gay, and now you don't seem to mind it. What's different?*) and from helping them shore up their repertoire of responses to kids who like to make other boys' business their own. Kudos to the kid—gay or straight, boy or girl—who calmly retorts: *Who I am and what I do isn't a problem for me. Why is it such a problem for you?*

TALKING TO YOUR SON ABOUT GENDER
STEREOTYPES AND PREJUDICE

The Teaching Tolerance program of the Southern Poverty Law Center, a nonprofit civil rights organization dedicated to fighting hatred and bigotry in Montgomery, Alabama, seeks to foster school environments in which children reject hate, embrace diversity, and respect differences. Among its many lesson offerings is one designed specifically to reduce gender stereotyping and homophobia in sports. Students are asked to identify and discuss homophobia and gender stereotyping in athletics, and think about how they can combat these attitudes and behavior at their own schools. Grade school children are asked to identify qualities that they associate with male and female athletes and the attitudes they have about gender, sexual orientation, and athletics. Middle and high school students read articles such as "Can the NFL Tackle Homophobia?"[3] and follow it up with completing handouts and keeping journals. Everyone is asked to discuss how stereotypes about gender and sexual orientation show up at his or her school and what ideas they each have for battling homophobia and gender stereotyping within their respective schools.

Parents can borrow from this program to introduce conversations at home about gender stereotypes and the prejudices that show up in school or while playing sports or even in their own kitchens and backyards and living rooms. For example, they can ask their kids what qualities they associate with male athletes. What about female athletes? How do they account for any differences? There are reasonable as well as prejudicial reasons for differences in a person's characterization of male versus female athletes; can they (or the parent) distinguish between them? What are some of the stereotypes people hear about male and female athletes? How do those stereotypes show up at their kids' schools? Broadening the conversation, parents can ask for and offer their own examples of how stereotypes harm as well as limit people, and talk about the attitudes they've come to have about gender, sexual orientation, and athletics.

In the 2006 Winter Olympics, a young man by the name of Johnny Weir competed in men's figure skating. Weir skated beautifully in his short program, but not so well in the long program. He didn't win a medal, despite high hopes from his countrymen. But his flamboyant style and unapologetic demeanor captured the attention and interest of viewers. And while his sexual orientation became cocktail-party chatter (the *Chicago Tribune* even took a poll about it), young people were drawn to his authenticity and candor with regard to his personal struggle to remain faithful to his unconventional style in a sport that prizes convention.

"Figure skating is thought of as a female sport, something that only girly men compete in . . ." Weir's website was quoted as saying during this time.[4] In his article, "Weir's Sizzle Fizzles," *Philadelphia Inquirer* columnist Phil Sheridan noted that for weeks Weir had been saying he wanted to be a role model for young people who felt they didn't fit in—kids who weren't on the football team or hanging out with the popular crowd. Weir himself had been one of those kids, bullied by boys playing hockey on the same ice where he would practice his figures; these bullies found it entertaining to watch Johnny dodge the hockey pucks they sent his way. However, Weir, temperamentally defiant and confident to the point of being brazen, was not a kid to be scared off the ice. It was in fact to Weir's grounded comfort with himself, as well as his frankness, that Sheridan attributed his sudden rise in popularity during the media's coverage of the Olympics.

> "Every little boy should be so lucky to turn out like me. That's what I think."
>
> Olympic figure skater Johnny Weir

Weir's popularity came at a price, however, that being the snide casting of suspicion about his sexual orientation. Granted, Johnny Weir played up his flamboyance and toyed merrily with the media, fanning the flames until they threatened to trump the attention he was getting for his skating. But the alacrity with which viewers jumped on the "are you or are you not gay" bandwagon is not only startling but very telling about the near-instantaneous assumptions people make about a boy's choice of recreation and his sexual orientation.

Weir hadn't known about the *Chicago Tribune* poll. "I think it's funny that people care," he said. "Something like that. It's not a big deal. Who I sleep with doesn't affect what I'm doing on the ice or what I'm doing in a press conference." Weir hit a chord with a lot of young people during those Olympic games, just as he'd hoped to do; over the three days he performed, his website in-box went from twenty-five fan e-mails to nearly nine hundred.

Weir reminds me of Chris Colfer, who plays the character of gay teen Kurt Hummel on Fox's television hit *Glee*. Kurt has been called one of the "most socially relevant characters on TV" in *Entertainment Weekly*, and Colfer reports getting fan mail from kids saying his poignant portrayal of Kurt has saved their lives or made them feel less alone. Featured again in *Entertainment Weekly* only seven weeks later, Colfer was joined by other young actors portraying gay teens on TV, where producers and networks are said to be trying to provide inspiration for their young viewers whose personal and social struggles have been ignored for years, only to be catapulted to the front pages of the news with a recent rash of bullying-induced suicides by young gay men.

On any given day, the sculpted faces of men known for their athleticism or physical prowess smile, stare, or sulk handsomely at us from our magazine pages, television screens, and computer monitors. Men recognized publicly for their empathic or aesthetic sensibilities are fewer in number. Fewest of all, however, are guys in the public eye who are featured for their compelling physicality and aesthetic sensibilities at the same time.

Michael Madsen, an actor perhaps best known for portraying the blood-soaked villain in *Kill Bill Volume 2*, steps up nicely, though. Interviewed in *Men's Health*, this father of five boys and author of two books of poetry had this to say about balancing the "tough" and the "tender" in his life:

> *My mother gave me culture. She encouraged me to be a sculptor and to read. And from my dad I got, "Ya gotta be the toughest son of a gun on the street." So I had this bizarre duality. I encourage my boys to do stuff in the arts, but I'm also a big advocate of not taking any sh——. I have a heavy bag [at my house in Montana], and every morning the boys go three 3-minute rounds on the heavy bag with the gloves.*[5]

For too many guys, though, these two ideals—tough and tender—are treated as if magnets of the same pole, forever estranged by their mutually repulsing forces. Men can be one or the other, but never both. Think of the anxiety surrounding guys getting married or becoming fathers, and all that's made of having over-the-top bachelor parties and last hurrahs. It's as if men are preparing to leave behind the richest and most emblematic experiences of malehood.

But *where exactly* is this conflict between tough and tender? Maybe nowhere, really. Maybe it's just an artifact of how we think about men and who they are and how they think and feel—a self-fulfilling prophecy with disabling consequences.

I've known mothers to worry about how they were going to

raise their sons lovingly while also preparing them to succeed in a rough-and-tumble male culture. Here again we run headlong into this same supposed conflict—being brought up with devotion and affection (the tender) and being taught the skills believed necessary to succeed in a competitive and often unforgiving, aggressive culture.

Loving children fiercely and boundlessly will not make boys soft. It will make them secure. And if boys need anything to make it in this world, it is security. I once knew of a father who would make his infant crawl across the room to get to his bottle. He believed that he was helping his young son to be prepared for what he described as a "tough world out there." It's reminiscent of the northern Pakistani Pakhtun proverb cited by David D. Gilmore in his book *Manhood in the Making: Cultural Concepts of Masculinity:* "The eye of the dove is lovely, my son, but the sky is made for the hawk. So cover your dovelike eyes and grow claws." [6]

There are places in the world and in our neighborhoods that require high levels of vigilance, a cool exterior, and an ability to hurt or even kill somebody in order to defend your own life or the lives of loved ones. But what happens outside the home is different from what can be allowed to happen inside a home; boys whose caretakers withhold what they instinctively seek and need become angry, resentful men. Yes, they can fight, but they may not be easily able to love.

Perhaps the seeming challenge is a result of a blurring between what it means to give love and give an exemption. Mothers who "love too much" may be mothers who *give in too much,* who look the other way too much, who lower the standards of acceptable behavior for their sons too often for reasons that might appear justified at the time (*he was just kidding, he has a hard enough time as it is with his dad gone, he just gets so difficult when I put my foot down*...) but turn out to be poor excuses for behavior that will probably grow worse with time.

People who feel they have enough of the essential things in life (nutrients, warmth, affection, protection, security) are available to other people in ways they could never be if they were still trying to get their fill. Like those who are actualizing their way through humanistic psychologist Abraham Maslow's hierarchy of needs, at each new level they become freer from the burdens of basic survival, comfort, and security, and then from the anxiety of not belonging or not being loved. Animals who have never known hunger are able to eat together peacefully.

By helping parents, other caregivers, and educators differentiate between loving unconditionally and relieving children of responsibility, we may enable more of them to show their affections unabashedly. And by helping them to recognize when and how to hold children accountable for their choices while simultaneously demonstrating their compassion and willingness to help, we may be able to reconcile the wishes of mothers who want to love their sons as they need their mothers to love them, while still preparing them to lead contented, successful lives.

From Either/Or Thinking to Both/And: Expanding Definitions of What It Means to Be Male

"The Tyranny of the Or" is how Jim Collins and Jerry Porras, authors of *Built to Last: Successful Habits of Visionary Companies*, describe the experience of facing two seemingly contradictory concepts and believing you must choose only one *or* the other but never both. Thus, businesses can be either effective or efficient, and health care providers can either run a lucrative practice or stay true to altruistic ideals. *He's one cool macho dude—but I can't imagine he'd be the first one you'd call when your dog dies* would be an example of how it plays out in the realm of gender expectations or roles, as would *He sounds like a nice, sensitive guy—but I kinda like them on the buff side . . .*

Among the younger set, it shows up like this: *Dude,* one wide receiver says to another, *what's up with all the books? I never took you for a "reader-type,"* or, *Why would you tell her you were sorry?* a too-cool-for-school eighth grader asks his compadre, on the assumption that being kind or civil cancels out any coolness factor one would have had.

As an alternative to this compromising kind of either/or thinking, Collins and Porras trumpet "The Genius of the And"—a way of accommodating what would appear to have been irreconcilable objectives or views. Thus, with some creative thinking and a flexible perspective, businesses have opportunities to become both effective and efficient, and health care providers can run successful practices that reflect their humanitarian ideals. Our cool macho dude is able to be recognized as the go-to person when you need a warm shoulder to cry on, the girl who likes her guys buff doesn't balk at the mention of a kind man, no one riding the travel team bus thinks twice when a young wide receiver pulls out novel after novel, and our punky middle schooler discovers that his sidekick is kind of a classy guy. Viva la package deal.

From Both/And to Transcendence: More Than Being Male or Female, We Are Human

Competence and compassion. Ambition and affection. These traits or aptitudes and others like them are often associated with one gender or the other. Those having to do with doing, acquiring, winning, competing, and dominating go in the male pile. The ones that have to do with caring, nurturing, and mending go in the girl pile. There's a lot of crossover of course, but at first blush, it's the boys who are ambitious and the girls who are affectionate.

The concept of "gender proteanism"—author Michael S. Kimmel's term for a temperamental and psychological flexibility that allows a person to adapt to his or her environment with a full range of emotions and abilities—seems the perfect antidote to the compromising attribution of traits to one gender *or* the other. In his book *The Gendered Society,* Kimmel writes about traits such as competence and affection, and others that are commonly labeled either "masculine" or "feminine," as being *distinctly human qualities* (italics mine), "accessible to both women and men who are grown up enough to claim them." I love this eloquent nod to the importance of acknowledging, at least every once in a while, our common denominator. It's just like what Beth deduced one of the mornings we sat together over coffee: "In humanity, there is no gender."

The notion of a "protean self," a "self that is mutable and flexible in a rapidly changing world," was first advanced by psychologist Robert Jay Lifton, author of *The Protean Self: Human Resilience in an Age of Fragmentation.* Said by Lifton to emerge most frequently under conditions of confusion or some other type of psychological unmooring, a person's protean self is what allows him to embrace, rather than be overwhelmed or undone by, the contradictions and complexities he might have to face in his life. It lends resiliency, and allows what would be experienced as only disruption to become something on the order of a personal evolution. By writing about us as living beings who differentially share a single set of personal qualities, Kimmel has helped us find what is most universal about ourselves, reminding us of another plane on which we can connect. Lifton's articulation of our often-unwitting internal process of recurring adaption and evolution helps us find what is most unique about ourselves. We can afford to forget neither one.

What would happen if we looked at the empathic and nurturing and aesthetic sensibilities exhibited by men as a natural outgrowth of mankind's centuries-long departure from evolutionarily driven roles? Sprung from the duties of feeding and protecting, men can now afford to do (and be) other things. And, referring once more to Maslow's hierarchy of human needs, there, on the top of the pyramid, on the highest level, are creativity, playfulness, aesthetic needs, and transcendence, among others. Looking at it through this lens, strong empathic or artistic faculties seen in men wouldn't be seen as traits "borrowed" from females, but as part of "legitimate" male behaviors in their own right, access to which became available to men as society moved through the ages to its present state. Our accepting this reframing of these kinds of unconventional male behaviors as the actualization of higher-level human needs would be a huge step toward creating more equitable social climates in which to raise our sons as well as releasing them from the straitjackets of gender stereotyping.

CHAPTER SEVEN

We Need a Different Type of Warrior

Mahatma Gandhi. Leonard Bernstein. Nelson Mandela. Heroic in their own ways, these great men presented without the machismo typically associated with "real" boys or "manly" men. They also stood behind values commonly thought of as feminine in nature—empathy, diplomacy, artistry, introspection. Nonetheless, they are all heroes, with great moral or intellectual force, each one having made singularly notable contributions to our world.

In his review of the book *Manliness,* in which author Harvey Mansfield explores the relevance of being considered manly in a society that has been working toward deemphasizing gender differences, *Philadelphia Inquirer* staff writer Art Carey makes a point of distinguishing between guys who evidence a manly style and guys who exude a manly essence. As an example of the latter,

Carey identifies none other than Fred Rogers, the children's television icon, who taught through poignant example about the healing power of caring, respect, and community. For Carey, Rogers's moral force was extraordinary. Indeed, all anyone has to do to grasp the understated power this man had to engage and influence is watch Rogers in his 1969 appearance before the United States Senate Subcommittee on Communications, where he spoke in support of continued funding for PBS and the Corporation for Public Broadcasting. In his six minutes of testimony, Rogers's earnestness, conviction, and grace stood up stunningly to the gruff impatience of subcommittee chairman Senator John O. Pastore, transforming him from cynic to unabashed supporter. "Looks like you just earned the $20 million," the senator told Rogers when he was done, to the cheering applause of the hundreds in attendance.[1]

Moreover, to underscore how genuine authority has nothing to do with the size of a person's biceps, and is immediately and universally recognizable, consider this excerpt in *Esquire* magazine from Tom Junod's account of Fred Rogers accepting the Lifetime Achievement Award during the 1997 Daytime Emmys:

> *Mister Rogers went onstage to accept the award—and there, in front of all the soap opera stars and talk show sinceratrons, in front of all the jutting man-tanned jaws and jutting saltwater bosoms, he made his small bow and said into the microphone, "All of us have special ones who have loved us into being. Would you just take, along with me, ten seconds to think of the people who have helped you become who you are. Ten seconds of silence." And then he lifted*

his wrist, looked at the audience, looked at his watch, and said, "I'll watch the time." There was, at first, a small whoop from the crowd, a giddy, strangled hiccup of laughter, as people realized that he wasn't kidding, that Mister Rogers was not some convenient eunuch, but rather a man, an authority figure who actually expected them to do what he asked. And so they did. One second, two seconds, seven seconds—and now the jaws clenched, and the bosoms heaved, and the mascara ran, and the tears fell upon the beglittered gathering like rain leaking down a crystal chandelier. And Mister Rogers finally looked up from his watch and said softly, "May God be with you," to all his vanquished children.[2]

Displays of power like Rogers's that have nothing at all to do with brawn also show up in the political arena. Weary of the bravado and "jocklike bluster"[3] that characterized the 2000–2008 Bush administration, our nation chose for its next president a man better recognized for his forthrightness, circumspection, and gracious humor than for his grandstanding and muscle flexing. Barack Obama's tact and ability to project hope helped him become a compelling enough figure to override America's uncompromising bias toward leaders who always walk and talk tough. He seemed a genuine candidate for brokering peace.

> "A boy doesn't have to go to war to be a hero; he can say he doesn't like pie when he sees there isn't enough to go around."
>
> Edward W. Howe

Pointing out the one hitch with this optimistic picture is William Bryan, the Lionville, Pennsylvania, massage therapist from earlier in the book. In one of our several conversations about masculinity, he said to me, "It all sounds good, but remember, *peacemaking is not an athletic quality.*"

Bryan grew up a nonathletic kid in a very sports-oriented community, and fought hard against the prejudices of teachers and phys ed instructors who held steadfast to their belief that sports were indispensable for boys. He hopes that educators and other prospective mentors of children not only have, but will find ways to demonstrate, a better appreciation of all the different dimensions to human experience and expression. "There's the political, economic, athletic, musical, and artistic," he said. "The problem isn't the fact that there are all these distinctions; other cultures don't have the problems we do integrating boys who aren't jocks. The problem is the elitism that the athletic community seems to feel entitled to demonstrate, and that our society at large seems to endorse."

Maybe peace making isn't an athletic quality, but it can be noble. And noble's pretty cool. Historical writings are laced with references to discipline and integrity and honor as manly qualities. Brett McKay, a law school graduate turned blogger who writes "The Art of Manliness" and who, along with his wife, Kate McKay, wrote *The Art of Manliness: Classic Skills and Manners for the Modern Man*, says that "[f]or thousands of years, being a man meant being honorable, having courage, having competence" and that "[t]ill the 1950s, manliness meant action and a force for good." Nobility certainly characterized gentlemen from the Victorian era, which extolled the virtues of honesty, courage, and politeness, virtues that, according to Christina Sommers in *The War Against Boys*, "are as important to the well-being of a young male today as they were in nineteenth-century England." And if we go even further back, to the era of the classic Athenian philosophers, we can hear in Plato's writings the echoes of lessons about civic-spiritedness and the cultivation of the soul he had learned from his mentor and teacher, Socrates.

Plato was offering the young men of his time an alternative ethic and lifestyle to the disharmony and hedonism celebrated by the epic poets of that era, an ethic characterized by a collective concern for the common good and a desire to live a rational, orderly life. "Being a guardian [of the common good] probably isn't as much fun as being the wild, moody, beautiful and charismatic demi-god of youth Achilles," comments Waller R. Newell, in his introduction to Plato's "How a Grown Man Should Live." "But, while Socratic manliness may not match the glorious excesses of Achilles's daring, neither does it lead to the adolescent self-pity, fury, and pointless aggression of his lot." Waller adds, "Under Socrates' influence, 'courage'—which in ancient Greek was literally a synonym for 'manliness'—becomes primarily a quality of soul, mind, and will, not of brute strength or martial prowess."

There does seem to be a bit of a return to class and gallantry in America. In a 2010 *Philadelphia Inquirer* piece about "Manning Up," Lini S. Kadaba and Elizabeth Wellington each wrote about how the age of the "metrosexual" man, identified by his vanity, excessive consumption, and generally softer-edged emotionality, has come and gone, in favor of what is being called the "retro-sexual." Retrosexuals want to put the man back in manhood, but keep it upscale. Think Don Draper of *Mad Men*.

Still, retrosexual smacks of affectation. Maybe what we miss are guys we can refer to as gentlemen. It sounds so old-fashioned, but it's my best way of describing an educated (but not academic), informed (but not pedantic), judicious (but not constricted), benevolent (but not Pollyanna-like), and personable (but not glib) man. The term depicts a way of life as much as it does a particular image; it's an ethic, really, something that shapes a man's attitudes, and in turn, guides his behavior. Cardinal Newman said it in this way: "It is almost the definition of a gentleman that he is one who never inflicts pain"[4]

Here's an example: A boy goes off to college and begins a relationship with a girl. They choose together to hold off for a little while on becoming sexually active. At a party, the boy is propositioned by another girl whom he knows casually. When his dorm mates discover that he declined her advances, they tease him relentlessly. "What! Are you kidding me?" they exclaim. "That's what college is for, you idiot!" Well, not for everyone. This boy's choices reflect his character, not his masculinity, and that's exactly the point we need to be making to boys today.

The quality of circumspection, and of self-restraint in the face

> **"Don't just be a gentleman, but a gentle man."**
>
> Mother of twenty-six-year-old Francis E. Crippen from Pennsylvania, who, in October 2010, died off the coast of the United Arab Emirates during the FINA Open Water 10K World Cup competition, *Philadelphia Inquirer*, October 31, 2010

of apparent opportunity, can be very sexy. They tell you that a person is discriminating, which means that he (or she) finds value in making the right choice from among different options. What does that have to do with being sexy? It implies that the person feels he can afford to wait for the right or most desirable option to present itself. It's a powerful message of self-respect— one of the sexiest characteristics a person can have.

The Understated Power of Pop Culture

Let's start with something simple: men hugging. Hugging "simply isn't a part of the masculine gender role," says Kory Floyd, associate professor of communication at Arizona State University, cited in Cynthia Hubert's article about the current wave of men hugging men.[5] "We socialize men to compete," he adds, "not to be affectionate." Documenting the types and lengths of hugs between men, Floyd found that they rarely involve full body contact or last more than a second. "Full-on hugs for most guys are pretty tricky," says Patrick Carone, entertainment director for *Stuff* magazine, also cited in the article. "Unless you just pitched a no-hitter or something like that, you don't get one, except maybe at a wedding or a funeral, and only among family." Other exceptions to the rule include the men on *The Sopranos*, adds Hubert, surmising that being a professional killer gives you a bye.

But a few years ago, men hugging men became—if not all the

rage—then at least okay, even fashionable. There were unspoken rules, of course: The hugs had to be brief, and involve minimal bodily contact. Backslaps and guttural noises were encouraged. This type of hugging seemed to have been started with "pound hugs" or "pound shakes" introduced by hip-hop artists. Celebs soon followed. Before we knew it, men all over the country were doing it. "You can walk into a Cheesecake Factory in the Midwest and see guys with their girlfriends greeting other guys with hugs. It's interesting and rather uplifting, I think," says psychotherapist and pop-culture commentator Joshua Estrin.[6]

So, it's not *impossible*, after all, to bend some of the gender norms that tell our boys (and girls) what they can and can't do. To do it, we just need public figures with whom the target audience can identify. Carone mentions that hugging got another big boost when the guys of HBO's show *Entourage*—the "cool guys who rule Hollywood"—start hugging each other as their way of demonstrating friendship or forgiveness. Not surprisingly, the cooler you are, the wider margin you get for "nonnormative" behavior.

Even venues such as ABC's *Dancing with the Stars* have been helpful in pushing the envelope regarding what is acceptable "manly" behavior. *Philadelphia Inquirer* columnist Annette John-Hall describes her intrigue with the appearance on the show of such sport icons as boxer Evander Holyfield and NFL receiver and Hall of Famer Jerry Rice. John-Hall reports that in the decade she spent covering sports, it was rare for her to encounter an athlete with his public guard completely down; after all, he had a macho image to protect. Seeing Rice shimmying in tight polyester slacks and platform shoes meant for her a broadening of today's narrow definitions of manhood, and this translated into a glimmer of hope that these few models of macho men who didn't fear ridicule might help shift the rigid and destructive mind-set among young men with regard to acceptable gender behaviors.

John-Hall goes on to point out that the African-American community especially is in need of redefining macho, which, for many of our nation's young black males, means maintaining an image (the cool pose: no emotions, no proper English, no attending school) for which they pay an incalculable price. Widely admired and a big moneymaker in pop culture, this cool pose, notes John-Hall, plays a major role in why these males are killing each other at nine times the rate of white youth.

"If you back down, you're a punk," says Mark Anthony Neal, explaining why certain African-American boys and young men would feel compelled to follow the edicts of a culture that could spell their demise. Neal is a professor at Duke University and the author of *New Black Man*, which attempts to lay out a new, less restrictive model of black masculinity. Neal points out that in the culture of young black males, negotiation is a sign of weakness. "Everything has to be a confrontation."

Not only is this message of the cool pose reinforced by the culture of hip-hop and sports' trash talk, it comes from "the top," Neal adds, ". . . from the White House." "Say what you want about [White House] policies, one of Bush's successes was getting across the message that a real man never wavers. You attack first . . . before they attack you."

New Role Models with New Stories

Few people would disagree that role models, fictional or not, can have a strong influence on how people conduct themselves and decide the relative value of their personal ideals. Consider Gregory Peck's Atticus Finch. In the wake of *To Kill a Mockingbird*'s popularity, the character of father-lawyer Finch—an indestructible man who ironically shares his name with one of the more delicate bird species—is recognized as a standout for integrity. As a larger-than-life figure, he's up for grabs by anyone wanting a picture of what it truly means to have character.

The best role models arise organically—people in the news or movies or, on a smaller scale, from one's circle of acquaintances and colleagues who very naturally come to symbolize certain values or manners of being that others then find inspirational and try to emulate. Nobody declared Atticus Finch a role model. He just *became* one because so many people responded to his brave displays of conviction and kindness, and marveled at his understated power to assert a semblance of justice in the face of rock-ribbed, blinkered bigotry.

But, honestly, while *we* love Atticus Finch, how many of our kids do? If we want to be successful in providing credible alternatives to the macho ideal, we need multiple, viable role models with whom young boys can—or better, *want*—to identify. The truth is that you can declare someone a role model all you want, but without a buy-in from those whom it is hoped the person will influence, he or she remains just another laudable public figure.

Still, we don't have to wait around for great role models to appear in the public landscape. Some live with us right at home. William Pollack, author of *Real Boys: Rescuing Our Sons from the Myths of Boyhood*, writes that in contrast to the myth that boys' heroes are distant Olympian figures such as sports stars, astronauts, and action-movie heroes, his own research showed that most teenage boys cite family members as heroes—brothers, sisters, moms, and dads. So, our own behavior, and the behavior we encourage in our homes, can serve as terrific examples.

At the same time we can continue to find movies or books or events that show males in different kinds of leadership roles besides those based upon athleticism or other blatantly powerful traits. Without making it too obvious that you have a motive beside entertainment, slip in a film like *Twelve Angry Men* every once in a while, or *A Raisin in the Sun*, where heroism is determined not by might but by candor, honor, a willingness to be proved wrong. Talk about a man like Tony Dungy, former head coach of the Tampa Bay Buccaneers and the Indianapolis Colts, and the first African-American coach to win a Super Bowl. Dungy's belief in the power of communion to inspire athletes and elicit great performances stood in brave contrast to conventional NFL wisdom about how to win football games. "I said we're going to win because we're going to create a family atmosphere . . . not everybody related to that," said Dungy in a 2007 interview for *Newsweek*. I bet not. Talk to your kids about how people can use words as weapons instead of fists. Give examples of where one person trumped another solely by virtue of wit or patience or restraint, any of which might be qualities your son or nephew or student exhibits. A favorite example of mine is *Glee* actor Chris Colfer's account of fighting back in high school when taunted with gay slurs: "One time I was walking and some-one said, 'F—!' and I turned back and said, 'Yeah, but can you spell it?'"[7]

Well-known personalities with their public platforms are invalu-able for raising the consciousness of large populations about wor-thy causes, human communities in need, and social trends that will bring us closer to our cultural ideals. But the most influential people in children's lives remain the adults who are closest to them and have the most contact with them. Fathers would seem an obvious choice of role model for their sons, and I believe most see themselves in that way. But several authors have explored what many see as a disturbing trend among young men, includ-ing those who are or would be fathers. In *The Decline of Men: How the American Male Is Tuning Out, Giving Up, and Flipping Off His Future,* author Guy Garcia describes men who, having lost their traditional roles as provider and protector, flirt with hollow sub-stitutes. He gives as examples the movie *Jackass* and gangster cultures, in which men pretend to be boys and boys pretend to be men, respectively. These unfortunate choices of substitutes for what males mean to a community have redefined manhood away from such things as compassion, responsibility, and family. Gary Cross, in his book *Men to Boys: The Making of Modern Immaturity,* talks about guys caught up in the "cynical thrill culture of the boy-man" in which they fixate on youth and chase the vacuous thrills of instant gratification only to end up living cynical, morally bankrupt lives.

For Cross, the idealization of youth and rejection of the traditional notions of mature masculinity, with its commitments and related responsibilities, have compromised men's abilities to serve as role models and mentors to their sons and other young males. He calls out for new stories that favorably explore growing up and being a grown-up, and can advance a culture that values accumulated experience, cultivated taste and conversation, and other unhurried pleasures (the slow food movement, gardening, hiking, collecting), similar to what Willard Spiegelman wrote about in *Seven Pleasures: Essays on Ordinary Happiness,* his contemplation on the civilizing and civilized pleasures of such ordinary activities as reading, looking, swimming, or writing.

These ideals of refinement and sagacity, and the appreciation of gratifying sensory pleasures, furnish a beautiful counterpoise to our nation's hyperkinetic, cacophonous culture where, in order to get anyone's attention, you have to be louder, bigger, and brasher than the others. These are the new stories we need, with their quiet, unsung heroes. We need whenever possible to be teaching boys that there are many ways to be a man, that, as Dan Kindlon and Michael Thompson say in *Raising Cain: Protecting the Emotional Life of Boys,*

> *[T]here are many ways to be brave, to be a good father, to be loving and strong and successful. We need to celebrate the natural*

creativity and risk taking of boys, their energy, their boldness. We
need to praise the artist and the entertainer, the missionary and
the athlete, the soldier and the male nurse, the store owner and the
round-the-world sailor, the teacher and the CEO. There are many
ways for a boy to make a contribution in this life."

Supplanting a Negative Role Model

For all the positive influence a role model can have on a person, there is too its flip side. A therapist once sought me out for help with one of her clients—a twelve-year-old boy caught in the cross fire of his parents' ugly divorce. The dad was aggressive and quick to intimidate with his large size and bellowing manner. He modeled a masculinity that was physical in nature and fed on power.

Much in the manner of his father, the boy was now beginning to bully his mother by challenging her authority in ways that made her appear incompetent. He also was deftly exploiting her wish to have any residual conflict in the household disappear. The boy rejected all attempts by the therapist to impose some degree of security and stability in the mother's custodial home, and spoke only of being able to muscle his way through any situation. "I'm the man of the house now," he said to the therapist, in his mother's uncontesting presence.

Seeking advice on how to temper this boy's bossy aggressiveness, the therapist shared with me the mother's account of a recent car ride in which a random aggressive driver cut her off, forcing her out of her lane, and her son's startling reaction to this: "The mom said he had his seat belt unbuckled and was ready to jump out of the car and go after this guy!" she relayed, adding, "He's *twelve*, Janet. What do I do to help him?"

I recommended to the therapist that the next time the boy came for a session, she go back to his comment about being man of the house. "I'd say to him that I understand he wants to be the man of the house, and that his way of being that man—tough and gruff—is one way of doing it. But then I'd ask him if he had a backup plan, something he could use just in case he was in a situation where tough and gruff wouldn't work so well . . . you know, like with other kids who also liked tough and gruff but were a foot taller than him, or if he, let's say, was angry about something his grandpa, who he loves and respects, said."

I explained, too, that trying to get this kid to adopt a different perspective about what it means to be a man by talking about the "right" thing to do would doom the therapy. He'd see her as one more person to pass through before finally being left alone to do what he wants to do. The therapist would lose credibility for not respecting his message ("I do things this way and like it") and for thinking that she could in fact muscle her own point across ("There are other, more appropriate ways to act like a man that won't get you in trouble"). Well, sure there are, but is there anything about the boy's disposition indicating this would be an appealing alternative for him? I suggested to her instead that she evoke a beginning curiosity about how other guys do it. "Ask him who his heroes are and see if there's one in the pack, real or fantasy, who brings something other than brawn to the table. Then talk about it with him. Ask him if he thinks any of his heroes ever gets self-conscious or frustrated if he can't be totally in charge of things. If he says, 'But he's not a real person,' tell him to make up what he thinks the character would say. Get him to play with you with his imagination. It will lighten up the whole therapy, and give you more access to him. If he says he doesn't have heroes, or that your question is stupid, then just tell him what you think one of your own heroes would say, or about a time when you found yourself spellbound by someone's ability to use only words to leave a bully standing red-faced and speechless, handily trumped by a kid half his size." Sometimes, curiosity and mystery do more to stretch a person's narrow point of view than any lecture in the world.

What Kind of Different Warrior Do We Need?

Power assumes many forms—physical, overwhelming, fear inducing, elegant, or inspiring, among so many others. One person's hero is a thug who keeps a neighborhood safe from rival gangs, and another person's hero—Beth's ten-year-old son, Ethan, for instance—is Neil Armstrong, because he was "brave and willing to do something no one else would do." As a subject of study, *power* can supply educators and students, parents and their children, mentors, youth leaders, coaches, rabbis, priests, and ministers with innumerable points of departure for discussions about its different manifestations, people's desires for and misuses of it, the advantages and disadvantages of holding it, and how people—and especially kids—imbue and divest others of it. And because children are so often and expensively at the mercy of the interplay between various human social needs, it probably makes sense for us to better educate them about the dynamics of power, and how it shows up on the playground and in the cafeteria and at the birthday parties and on dates. Innocence here simply leaves a kid vulnerable to one of the worst kinds of power—the kind you don't even know exists. And it cuts short opportunities for kids to learn about power as a *positive* force, as something they can assume without violence or manipulation, and at no one's expense.

We need warriors today, not for fighting each other but for fighting hunger, discrimination, pollution, human slavery, and the abduction of children for soldiery, among many other conditions of human and animal suffering. We need warriors who can battle cogently and convincingly in boardrooms and in the media, in schools and courtrooms, in forgotten jail cells and in dusty fields long rendered infertile by poverty, pollution, or civil war. And we need leaders among these warriors who can match the nuanced complexions of these kinds of battles with an incisive intelligence, stellar communication skills, and a talent for moving fluidly between competing perspectives and entities.

What does all this have to do with a boy who doesn't like to play sports? It has a lot to do with him, or rather it can, because the call-up right now is for individuals who have at their disposal a variety of skills and emotionally affecting traits that are *not* rooted in the physical, the competitive, or the aggressive but that tap the more protective and generative dimensions of warriorship, such skills as:

Ethical sensibilities. Interestingly, for all the chatter and stereotyping about the "geeky" social interactions of intellectually gifted children, many have been noted as having advanced aptitudes regarding ethical and moral sensibilities. It makes sense: Moral reasoning is, if nothing else, abstract in nature, something at which smart, ideational people are good. And most social interactions during all but the last few years of high school typically don't involve big moral or ethical dilemmas, meaning that, in those earlier years, all those fancy skills may not count for much. But it is an interesting juxtaposition of skill and weakness: strong ethical sensibilities, gifted intelligence, and *supposed* average to low-average social skills. One explanation for this is offered by James Webb, Elizabeth Meckstroth, and Stephanie Tolan in their book *Guiding the Gifted Child*. They say that the rapid movement with which gifted kids travel through the different stages of moral development often leaves them out of step with their peers. Congruent with Beth's and my own impression that the talents and aptitudes of nontraditional boys often show up later than do the ones of traditional, physically expressive boys, the authors go on to say that, in their experience, while only about 10 percent of all people reach the highest stages of moral development, the majority of gifted children do. These individuals are found to adhere to a strong inner conscience and to several abstract, universal principles such as equality of all people, respect for human dignity, and a commitment to justice. The authors add that we can find among them the people who become "the leaders, creators and inventors in our society, making key contributions and often changing some of our major traditions in the process."[8]

Granted, boys who don't play sports should no more be *equated* with intellectually gifted boys than athletic boys should *not* be, but the point here is this: Educators can be alert to material into which matters of ethics and/or morality can be brought, so that kids with these kinds of sensibilities have more opportunities to stand out from the student body and be recognized for the distinct intellectual and philosophical contributions they can make. That some of those kids might be boys who have little interest in or aptitude for sports is an extra benefit, the primary being the teasing out and exposition of less visible, *non*physical talents in social-academic communities.

Ambassadorship. Ambassadorships often are filled with people who've learned to use their confidence and charisma to bridge the differences between people, cultures, and ideologies. But for some people, that kind of strong persona is intimidating or overwhelming. Instead of inspiring trust, it makes the other person uncomfortable, and less likely to be open to something or someone new and unfamiliar.

This is where a quietly natured person does what his more colorful counterpart cannot. In such a person's unassuming presence and stately presentation of competency, others allow themselves to be known and led, even if briefly. It's a good start.

At a conference years ago, I went to see another psychologist speak about doing therapy with children. He was a soft-spoken man, small-statured and bookish. He told a story about a time when one of his kids confessed some misdeed and, as a part of that, relayed the manner in which he had responded to his son, trying to help him understand his choice of actions. There was something about the unimpassioned, kind patience with which this man had listened to his son's account of what had happened that has me remembering to this day the reaction I had sitting in that lecture hall: *That's somebody I could see myself telling anything to.*

The capacity for awe and transcendence, and an appreciation of the value of personal presence. If you want to be able to affect the world, you need to be able to tolerate its affecting you, and that means allowing yourself to be moved by the human condition to the point of both tears and rapture. As part of teaching nonviolent communication, Boston-based martial-arts expert Jason Gould asks students to answer the question *What is alive in me?* I think of a person's response to that question as being capable of revealing his or her greatest instrument for affecting other human beings. It's the part of him or her that will touch, move, attract, inspire, quiet, or activate others—if given the opportunity. It's where a person has presence; it's a beautiful power.

But in order to know what's alive inside, a person has to be able to stop, and be still, and wait, and feel or listen to what it is that fills them with awe and benevolence and a wish to share that part of themselves with others. This is easier for the introspective, psychologically minded, or reverent person than it is for someone who lives in the physical and body-kinesthetic and whose way of interfacing with the world is through movement and action. The latter type is at risk of underestimating the value of *presence*—something that doesn't do, but rather *is*. Beth once said to me that what kids need is for their parents to stop talking, and sit down on the floor next to them, and wait quietly to see what comes up. I loved that, and knew then we'd be friends forever.

Not all warriors are heroes, but most heroes are warriors in some sense, having vanquished another's despair, apathy, or adversary. Heroes really can be anyone who makes the people around him or her feel bigger or better, or who helps them connect to their own humanity, or that of others. That's exactly what I saw two middle school cross-country runners do in a meet in which one of their teammates—heavier and considerably less fit than the others—had dropped way behind the pack. Gasping for breath, his running having slowed to a near walk, the boy was destined not only to finish last, but to finish a good minute or so after the last runner before him would finish. With the couple of hundred kids and parents and teachers there watching, this would no doubt have felt like an eternity. And so, turning around just yards from the finish line and noticing this, in silent accord these two other boys stopped and waited for their teammate to catch up to where they were, whereupon they linked their arms in his and, as a trio, walked through the finish line together.

CHAPTER EIGHT

Family Matters

Years ago I answered a call from the mother of a twelve-year-old boy whose quiet, composed nature had her and her husband thinking that he might be depressed or suffering from low self-esteem. I invited the whole family in for the initial session and was glad that I did, because it reminded me about the importance of context when trying to understand someone's behaviors, and the important role of the family in how children grow up to think about themselves.

Mark, it turned out, was a pensive, introverted adolescent growing up in a family of extroverts. He adored all three of his bright, bouncy brothers, and enjoyed their company—as long as it was in small, digestible chunks of time. Mark laughed at their raucous banter and bawdy jokes, and was proud of their many athletic accomplishments, but never really took center stage for himself. He was a behind-the-scenes kind of guy, happy to watch his brothers' games from the bleachers, spend an afternoon in the woods by his home, or simply read. In a lot of families, Mark would have been a regular, if not particularly sports-minded, kid. But in this family, he stood out like a sore thumb.

To me, Mark didn't seem depressed at all, or dissatisfied with either himself or his disinterest in sports. I started to think instead that having a son who was different from the type of boy they'd expected to raise challenged Mark's parents, and that they mistook their feeling challenged for Mark's being troubled. I shared these thoughts with Mark and his parents, and told them that one of the tasks of healthy families is welcoming the young men and women their children grow into. Could the parents see the value in making more room for Mark as an individual rather than hoping he'd conform to the picture of the family they'd been holding in their minds since they first thought about having children? Could they view him not as missing something his brothers had, any more than his brothers were missing something Mark had? And could the family do all this respectfully, without the patronizing humor that sometimes accompanies awkward transitions in family relations and mores?

Mark's brothers joined Mark and his parents for the next few sessions, and together the family worked their way through those questions and the others that grew out of them. On the day of the family's last scheduled session several weeks later, Mark's mother said something that told me she really got it. "You know," she started out, "I think it's not only the Marks of the world that need other people to understand there are a lot of ways to be a guy. It's really the whole world."

HELPING BOYS WHO DON'T LIKE TO PLAY SPORTS BY SHARING PERSONAL STORIES OF TRANSFORMATION

Therapy helped Mark's family respectfully recognize gender diversity and value of what Mark had to offer as a son and brother and young man who was different from his brothers. In many ways, the therapy was a microcosm of what needs to take place in the community at large. I'd like to believe that sharing these kinds of personal stories with friends, other relatives, or even close coworkers could play a small but important role in accelerating the sluggish pace of change that characterizes shifts in public opinion. The more often these stories of discovery and validation are told, the better illuminated our biases become, and the greater the gentle pressure to change them.

Fathers, Sons, and Sports

"Mama says I should throw the ball with you. Yah? You would like me to?"

I hesitate. This is a novel idea. My father and I have never played catch. The very notion makes me a bit nervous.

"Okay," I say.

"Where should I stand?" he asks me.

"Anywhere."

He takes a few steps away and turns to me, a look of almost pained concentration on his face, as if straining to hear.

I throw the ball to him. Startled, he stiffly brings his arms together. The ball plunks against his chest and he squeezes it there.

Underhand, he jerkily tosses it back in my direction, still with the deadly serious expression on his face.

"Throw overhand, Daddy."

Again, he heaves it to me underhand. Is anyone watching?

"Overhand, Daddy!"

"What's wrong like this?" He laughs, exasperated. Then again jerks the ball wildly in my direction. Underhand. Overhand. How can anyone take this seriously? Isn't this the height of absurdity?

We look at each other.

"Vos vilst du fun mir?" he pleads, throwing his hands in surrender. What do you want from me?

And suddenly I know he doesn't want to be doing this. Neither do I. It's not working. I hold on to the ball, turning it over in my hand.

"Thank you, Daddy. Let's stop. Never mind." I turn and go into the bungalow, leaving my father standing in the fading light, his hands at his sides, bewildered.

So much for playing catch. We never try it again.

This story vividly portrays the sad and often touching drama that unfolds when people try so hard to connect in the "right" way that they lose, if only for those moments, the ability to connect at all. It comes from *The Way Home: Scenes from a Season, Lessons from a Lifetime,* Henry Dunow's memoir about growing up with parents who saw no value in sports, and trying to connect with his own young son through the shared experience of Little League.

Many men will credit sports as having served as a cornerstone of their relationship with their fathers by way of providing an easy backdrop for talking and enjoying each other's company. They look forward to carrying on the tradition with their own children. But when their sons show little interest in the rudimentary rituals of bonding, such as playing catch or shooting basketballs, with their marked trails for relating, these fathers are left to come up on their own with other templates for connecting, or wing it altogether.

Some dads do better than others. A great many are disappointed by their son's disinterest, and allow it to show. Believing it to be a sign of weakness in their son or a failure on their part, they let their embarrassment overrule their better judgment. More than a few dads get downright angry and try to humiliate their sons into assuming a more aggressive or masculine manner, a coarse tactic that rarely ends well. The more diplomatic fathers try to mask their agenda, staging forced tickle games and wrestling matches that conclude with equally miserable results. *I tried*, some of these dads will say. *We just don't have anything in common.* Well, no, they won't have anything in common, as long as the father's interests serve to determine what is common ground. There's nothing that says to a child *I am committed to you and to us* more than a parent who offers to go way outside of his or her comfort zone in order to do their relationship justice.

The good news is that a lot of relationships start out rocky but get better over time. Apologies can be extended and affections renewed. Between willing parties, even severely fractured relationships can be repaired. Time brings with it not only opportunities for new conversations and ways of engaging but a broader perspective, enabling older children and their parents to move through impasses that years ago kept them apart. People who genuinely want to connect usually can find a way to do it.

Few dads ever really intend to hurt their non-sports-playing sons or cause them to feel any less loved than their siblings. Many are imprisoned by hand-me-down beliefs about what boys do and don't do or what boys need and don't need from their fathers. They are in desperate need of updates and of ways to transition from old to new. The best ones will come from other fathers who had similar reactions to their own nonathletic sons but discovered how not to let them interfere with the relationships they were trying to build. They will come also from fathers who didn't or couldn't protect their sons from their anger or disappointment, but who later on came back to them and said, *I am very, very sorry that I let you down by insisting sports were the only way we could ever relate. I want to try again, differently, and will need both your forgiveness and your help.*

Adult sons, too, can be the ones to come forward and initiate a second chance at assembling the kind of relationship that wasn't possible before. They can go back to their fathers and tell them that they want more for both of them, and that they're willing to do the work this might require: *Dad, I want us to be able to do more than talk superficially, and want to move past the difficulties and hurt feelings of years past. I think that when you realized*

I was never going to be the football-loving kid you expected me to be, you didn't know what to do. And I was too young to know how to tell you to keep trying to connect with me. I didn't want you to give up, but I thought I had disappointed you so badly that I didn't deserve to have you keep at it. I guess you felt bad about it all and I know I did, and I think we both just gave up. But I'd like another go at it, and think we can do better.

What if Dad disappoints again? If he disappoints because the man is not emotionally capable of handling the task of revisiting the past or of connecting without his customary defenses, then there's nothing to be gained by forcing the issue or trying to "guilt" him into compensating for his flawed efforts of years ago. I think it's better for a disappointed son to draw on his store of compassion and "mine" the relationship he actually does have with his dad for what *is* available—companionship maybe, shared memories, irrefutable love. However, a father who allows himself to disappoint because of self-protection or stubbornness or lack of interest disillusions his son. It's a tremendous loss—the fantasy of what still could be. But maybe what the disillusionment also does is free the son, presumably a young man, to grieve for what he now knows he'll never get from his father—ample approval, validation, affection—as well as for what he can't evoke from him—pride, and a genuine curiosity about and interest in who he actually is. Hopefully, he'll be able to always remind himself that the limitations of the relationship he and his dad share have to do with his dad's shortfalls, not his, and that as personal as it feels, it's really not personal to *him*. It remains personal to his *father*, whose insecurities and defensiveness gave safe harbor to his blind spots and partiality. The son's willingness to open his heart and risk again the pain of rejection or devaluation speaks volumes, however, about the man he himself has become, and I would only hope that from that he would derive some portion of the esteem he deserved all along.

When Dads Push and Moms Protect: Drawing Parents Back Toward the Middle Again

Frictions between sport-oriented fathers and their nonathletic sons almost always manage to seep outside the orbit of the father-son relationship and work their way into others. Mothers and fathers especially can find themselves polarized from each other as they become increasingly extreme in their opinions. Most of that has to do with their respective efforts to convince the other parent to change, or convince the other parent that he or she is an idiot. It all starts when a father, typically, insists his son play a sport (sometimes the father's sport). Sometimes he'll insist that his son excel at the sport as well. The boy obliges for a while, then resists. Dad is disappointed. The boy tries again but still doesn't like it. He becomes unhappy. Dad gets angry. Mom responds by "protecting" their son from the father's manhandling of the "problem." He complains about her turning his boy into a sissy, and she in turn calls him an insensitive brute.

Fourteen-year-old Dylan sat on a couch in my office sandwiched between his parents and he looked miserable. This was the O'Brien family's first appointment with me, and I could already feel the tension between Dylan's mom and his dad. What I didn't know was where it was coming from. I soon found out.

"Dylan is a great kid, but he's not been himself lately," Mrs. O'Brien began.

"What's he like when he's himself?" I asked, looking over at Dylan, who was listening with guarded interest.

"Well, he's happy and funny, likes to do a bunch of different stuff . . ." Dylan's mom replied. None of the different stuff, I soon learned, involved sports.

The O'Briens had been referred to me by Dylan's pediatrician. Not only had Dylan's grades been dropping, he seemed depressed as well. Shortly afterward, Dylan volunteered that he'd started scratching himself a little bit on the tops of his thighs.

Dylan was a very different kid from the boy his parents had expected to raise. He liked skinny jeans and colored Converse high-top sneakers. Dad wore wingtips. Dylan spent hours listening to obscure bands and wore black nail polish. Both of Dylan's parents—staunch traditionalists—tried hard to get Dylan into baseball. It didn't work.

In this first session, Dylan's dad tried to dismiss his son's aversion to sports as "no big deal," but it was obvious that Dylan's frank avoidance of any kind of competitive physical activity bothered him. At one point, Mr. O'Brien asked Dylan why he didn't even try to play. Dylan told him that he wasn't any good at baseball anyway.

"So? Learn to be better," admonished Mr. O'Brien. "Practice. Then you can try out for the team next year."

"Dad, I'm not interested in trying out for baseball," responded Dylan. "I don't want to play the game. Besides, it's too late anyway. The guys who play have been playing forever. They spend their weekends in batting cages. There's no way I'm going to get good enough in five months to play for a high school team."

"What do you mean it's too late?" asked Dylan's dad. He looked at Dylan as if Dylan were pulling excuses out of a hat. "When I was in eighth grade, I wanted to play football but I wasn't as good as the other kids, and you know what? I practiced. I practiced and worked really hard *and I caught up*."

I looked over at Dylan, who was just staring at the floor. He had nothing to say—but his mom did.

"Sean, Dylan's right," Mrs. O'Brien said. "Dylan can't just 'catch up.' It's different now. A lot of those guys have been playing since second grade. It's a lot more serious than it was when we were kids."

But for Mr. O'Brien, this was just one more way in which his wife overprotected their son. His waving of his hand spoke volumes: *There you go again, Eileen.* I figured it was time to weigh in. "Actually, I think Eileen is right," I said. "It really is different now. Most kids can pretty much learn anything they want to learn, but if you're talking about high school sports, it's just a whole different scene. By the time you've 'caught up,' they're already ahead again. And besides, *Dylan doesn't want to play*." I looked again over at Dylan, who was trying hard to look as if he wasn't listening. "I even think that talking about Dylan catching up sends the message that his not wanting to play is secondary to whether or not he should." I then turned directly toward Dylan's father and said, "There must be something very important to you about Dylan playing sports for his message to have been sidelined."

"I don't know," Mr. O'Brien softly replied, sitting back on the couch. But it turned out he did know, once he let himself think about why sports had become such a big deal in the family, at least for him. Mr. O'Brien began to describe how he had felt close to his son during Dylan's earlier years. Back then, they played a lot of physical games and shared some simple hobbies. Mr. O'Brien found it easy to enchant and amuse his son, and the two enjoyed their time together.

But as Dylan got older, he and his dad played together less and less. Interest in the hobbies waned, and talking became more difficult. Around the time of his preadolescence, Dylan was developing ideas of his own, many of which deviated from or opposed his father's. Their relationship began to change, triggering a lot of anxiety for Dylan's dad. He was worried that without sports to play and watch together—the male relationship staple—he and his son would drift further and further apart.

"I don't know what else we'd do together where we wouldn't end up disagreeing," Mr. O'Brien said.

"Have you ever told Dylan that you were worried about drifting apart?" I asked, looking over at the boy, who was watching us intently.

"No, I wouldn't want him to think that I believed it could ever happen."

"But you *do* believe it could happen, and that's not a dangerous thought. It's actually very moving. I think a child would feel touched to know his parent was thinking that much about their relationship. It says it really matters. The irony here is that your anxiety about drifting apart propelled you to force something that actually did start to drive you guys apart."

"So, what do I do?" Mr. O'Brien asked, appearing uncertain and totally without bearings.

"Sometime later tonight or tomorrow or whenever it seems right, tell Dylan exactly what you just told me, even though he heard you say it here. Ask him to join you in trying to stay connected when it seems all you can do is disagree with each other."

"And what if we can't?" Mr. O'Brien asked, staring straight at me. He was still too nervous to look over at his son. This was all foreign territory to him.

"Trying and failing and trying again is one way of staying connected," I said. "Maybe it'll be enough to carry you guys for a while until things change a little. *Your relationship with Dylan can still be good even though you may not share the same values or perspectives anymore.* It'll come down to respect. You don't need sports to do this, and you don't have them anyway. Let Dylan show you the young man he is becoming, and reciprocate by letting him see more transparently the man you've already become."

There was one more thing I still had to address—the competition between Sean and Eileen in relation to whose opinion better reflected Dylan's best interests when the issue of sports or physical activity came up. Directing my remarks to both parents but looking first at Sean, I added, "There's a bonus outcome to relieving your relationship with Dylan of the burden to be sports-related. I think that if Eileen knows you're listening to Dylan and not adamant about him playing a sport he doesn't want to play, she won't feel a need to 'protect' him. And," I continued, "I don't think that you'll feel such a need to push Dylan in a direction he doesn't want to go if you know and can trust that you have other ways to stay connected."

"How Do I Know If I'm Encouraging Him or Pushing Him?" Discovering What's Right for Your Son

You're getting ready to load your son and his gear into the car and notice that he's gone back into the house for what must be his fifteenth trip to the bathroom. When he comes out, his eyes are red and watery. He tells you that he doesn't feel well. *Does he have to go to basketball practice today?* he wants to know. It's the third time in five weeks that he's wanted to skip.

The situation shows up in a hundred different ways for thousands of parents on any given day, but one thing is always clear: Someone's child does not want to go to the practice/game/sport lesson of some kind. It's a big moment for everyone—the beginnings of either a protracted battle for power and control, or a family experiment in handling strong differences of opinion, balancing concerns for a child's welfare with respect for his wishes and individuality, and constructively managing a colorful mix of emotions.

There are dozens of questions that come up at this juncture and in the weeks or months that follow: whether or not to insist the child go; how to handle a tantrum; what it will mean if the child is allowed to skip one session or quit altogether; whether letting him avoid sports will be enabling his anxiety about competing/getting hurt, or demonstrating respect for his individuality; if it will be a problem getting into college without any sports listed on his high school transcript . . . There are few useful stock answers to these questions because each boy and family face a variety of issues. The same decision or response may be enabling for one boy but kind for another. Some boys need to be pushed a little at a time because without that they wouldn't do anything new. A more independent kid could feel so offended by being pushed that he digs in even harder or blows up at the parents.

Parents need something, though, to help them navigate all this. Whenever compiling a set of rules starts feeling forced, I look instead for the types of *questions* that can serve as guides for arriving at destinations with everyone's values and esteem and dignity intact. That, to me, seems the overall and most important objective; without those things still in place, I consider the price paid for any other accomplishment (he stuck the season out, he learned a new sport, he learned that he can do things he thought he couldn't, he made a new friend) too high. Here are four of these types of questions:

1. Are you affording your son ample opportunities to tell or show you who he really is and who he doesn't care to be?

2. Are you hearing him and does he know that you are hearing him? Check in with your son to make sure that what you heard matches what he told you. Remain present and focused on him during the entire time you're talking.

3. Are your actions and decisions communicating to your son that you respect him, and will largely follow his lead in giving shape and meaning to his life?

4. Are you finding ways of helping your son to understand that there might be times when you will want to push him in order that he doesn't get stuck in his comfort zone—not because you are trying to control his activities or friends?

5. Can you separate the objective (e.g., finding new friends, becoming a well-rounded individual) from the means by which it can be accomplished (sports versus other types of activities) so that some of the conflict is obviated altogether?

So . . . do I insist or not?

Your son is making it clear that he doesn't want to go. He might be adamant, anxious, even tearful. Saying to him *Okay, we'll pass on it* feels too soft and all but promises a repeat performance the next time your son's supposed to be somewhere he doesn't want to be. On the other hand, insisting he go—tears or panic or tantrum and all—feels too authoritarian, and downright unkind. What to do? Again, the chances of coming up with the "right" answer improve as the quality of the questions you ask yourself in the midst of these situations improves. Here are other examples of the types of questions that can help guide parents toward solutions in which kids don't feel muscled into activities any more than parents feel disabled from parenting their children.

1. What am I hoping to accomplish in this particular situation (avoid setting a precedent, showing my son who's in charge, showing him that I believe in him, keeping his dad from calling him names, getting him to try something new)?

2. How much of that will actually take place if my son and I are in conflict with each other?

3. Are there places where my objectives and my son's objectives overlap, and can be brought into play as good starting points?

4. Is my relationship with my son characterized by too much leniency and accommodation, suggesting that I need to better and earlier define what I think is critical for his growth and commit to following through on it?

5. Or have I been too rigid, not taking into account that my son is getting older, or alternatively, always thinking that I know what he needs better than he does just because my own parents used to make decisions that way?

6. Are there other ways to accomplish what it is I think is important for my son to experience (e.g., getting exercise, making friends, taking risks) than through sports or physical activity, or am I working too hard to avoid conflict over what shouldn't be a big deal?

7. If I "stick to my guns" here, what will I actually be accomplishing (maintaining my position as the one who is in charge, embarking on an ugly road with my son, causing him to lose faith or trust in me, getting him to a place where he can see that he is more capable than he believes he is, a combination of the above), and is it worth the potential rift in our relationship?

Let's go back to the kid who doesn't want to go to wherever it is he's supposed to be headed. A best-case scenario for insisting your son go is that he discovers, to everyone's surprise, that he likes this or that sport more than he thought he would, or that he is better at it than he had believed. A feeling of *Okay, I can probably do this* may be all the encouragement he needs in order to take it a little further—all of which will evaporate in the wake of a parent saying something along the lines of *Hey, I told you you'd like it!* or *See! You just had to stick with it!* Parents are often surprised to hear this—*What's wrong with saying that?* they challenge. *What? Am I just supposed to say nothing?*

No, not nothing—but certainly not *that*. Because as brief and well intentioned as the remark is, it is still going to offend the child. It says to him, *You see, I knew all along that this would happen. You should have just listened to me in the first place.* Which says, *I know what the outcome in these situations is going to be,* which is just another way of saying, *I really do know better about these things.* Maybe you do—but that's not what matters here. What matters is making sure your son doesn't feel embarrassed for doing something his parent were "right" about. And there's nothing that says *I respect you* more than choosing *not* to jump on an opportunity to say out loud that you were right and the other person was wrong.

A more supportive thing to say in these instances would be *Hey, nice job* or *That was terrific* or *Nice surprise to find out you're not half bad at that, isn't it? Good for you.* And then, instead of assuming your son will build on that experience by doing more, *ask* him what he wants to do next, as in, *Do you want to try this again?* or more strongly, *Hey, I'm hoping you'll use what happened today to try some other things you haven't wanted to try . . .* These kinds of remarks keep you and your child on the same side of the fence while tackling what has likely been, over the years, a thorny and contentious issue.

But what if the results aren't good: Your son falters, finds out that he really hates the activity, discovers he's as bad as he thought he'd be. What then? Move on to something else and appreciate that he tried. Probably the worst thing to do would be to insist he continue to play. He will not get much better and he sure won't hate it any less. If he's forced to get better by being signed up for a run of private lessons, then what you'll have is a miserable kid who plays a sport adequately. And the takeaway for him? *It is more important that he be marginally competent in an arena his parent has decided is important for him (socially, personally) than for the two of them to take the time to discover his genuine areas of competence, and more important, his genuine areas of interest.* The contested issue here is *not* parents' wishes to equip their sons with skills believed to be important for their growth and social well-being. It is the matter of respect. The intent may be very sound, but the means by which it is or isn't accomplished may or may not play out in a way the child recognizes as respectful.

Parents worry that by relenting they risk losing their credibility and power. If that happens, then it's more likely to be a function of the quality of the relationships within the family than the parents giving in. With a few exceptions, a person's credibility and power to influence loved ones are suitably robust to stand up to any one bad decision or action. I think parents in healthy relationships with their children stand to gain their respect and establish even greater credibility when they make such comments as,

- I'm not sure what to do here. I don't feel right making you participate in something that you so dislike, but it is important to me that you are involved in something outside the home where you have opportunities to interact with kids your age. Let's figure out a better solution.

- Sometimes it feels as though your dad and I are the only ones trying to find activities that you would enjoy. I think that if you would be a more active part of this process, and came up with some of your own ideas, it'd feel less like we're always trying to "shove sports down your throat," as you like to say . . .

- My concern with all this is only that you have some way to be physically active on a regular basis. If you could solve that piece of it, I'll cease and desist with the sports.

- What I'm really looking for you to do is to find new friends . . . but maybe it doesn't have to be through sports. Why don't you think about some other activities you'd be willing to try and we'll check them out?

- I just want you to have choices when you're around a large group of people. It bothered me to see you by yourself at Thanksgiving when all your brothers and cousins were playing football and other games in the backyard. I don't think you have to actually be in the game—it's just that you looked like you were avoiding them so they wouldn't be able to ask why you weren't playing, and that made me feel bad for you.

What do I do when he has a tantrum?

Let your son know that temper tantrums are not okay, and won't be nearly as effective in getting his point across as talking about what is so awful about playing. Insist that he find a better way to say, *I don't want to do this.* Be sure to impose some kind of consequence so that he doesn't do it again—at least without thinking about it. The consequence doesn't need to be punitive, just something that makes him question whether the tantrum was worth it. I like to call them consequences of restitution, or of inconvenience. For instance, if your son's temper tantrum causes his sister to be late for her dance lesson, he opts to either select one of her chores to do for her, or write her a note of apology. If he causes you to be late for something, or simply holds you up, ask for the time "back" by having him help you with something you needed done around the house. The issue isn't so much relating the "punishment" to the "crime" but rather addressing the fact that you are all part of a working, intimate community (a family) whose members depend upon one another to make things go smoothly, and when one person decides to indulge himself at the others' expense, he needs to give back to the community in some way.

Your son's tantrums may be bigger than the whole "I don't want to play sports" thing; it may be his customary way of handling frustration, and have a long history attached to it. Even if that's the case, this is as good an opportunity as any to help your child face the limits of his control over his life and the world.

On the other hand, consider that his tantrums may be a last-ditch effort to say, "WHY IS NOBODY LISTENING TO ME!"—in which case, after the tantrum is over and he's settled down, you might tell your son you're aware that when people feel really desperate to get their message out and feel no one has listened to them, they resort to anything in order to get someone's attention. Ask him if he feels as if no one is taking his point of view seriously, and then once you've asked him, sit back, commit to silence, and *listen*. Beth calls this "listening out loud," and it's something she taught her three boys so that others in their presence would always feel the privilege of being heard.

If we accommodate our son's wish to stop playing, will it be setting a precedent for all future circumstances in which he is reluctant to try something new?

Not necessarily, and nothing that a candid conversation and follow-through won't prevent. For example, *I didn't want to leave you in there because it was obvious you were miserable/it wasn't working out/it was getting worse/it was taking you in the wrong direction/you were very uncomfortable. But it's important to us that you understand that leaving a situation shouldn't be a first choice. I want you to be able to stick things out, even if they're uncomfortable—that, however, was just too much.*

Besides, it's a lot better to do *something* than leave a child in an untenable situation just so he "won't get the wrong idea."

Won't he need sports to get into college?

No. He'll just need to have done *something*. Too many kids are already spending two or three or more years signing up for activities in which they have little interest only because "it will look good on a college application." What little faith parents must have in the ability of their kids to project an enthusiasm and meaningfulness about their activities of genuine choice, and in the ability of admissions personnel to see it.

Doesn't he need to play sports in order to have friends?

No. If sports aren't your son's natural game, then that's not where he's going to find his friends.

Doesn't he need sports in order to feel good about himself?

Only if his value as a person has been defined, over the years, by how good he is on the diamond or basketball court. As his parents, you have a lot of control over that.

Sometimes my husband tries to embarrass our son into playing sports. Is this going to make it worse?

It's going to make *everything* worse. Being shamed into playing sports by his father will quash any smidgen of interest or goodwill that your son might have had. Worse, it will corrode any faith your son has in his father to respond to him as his own person instead of the person his father wants him to be. Another consequence of your husband's strategy is that it will not only vividly reveal his disappointment in his son, but force him to make an impossible choice between getting positive regard from his dad and retaining his personal dignity. Nothing good ever comes out of using shame to prompt change in someone else's behavior or attitude, and any "improvement" you see is likely to be short-lived, riddled with resentment, and terribly costly to the relationship.

My wife is overprotective—how can I get her to back off?

Your description of your wife as overprotective makes me wonder if she would in turn describe you as underprotective. Most likely, the two of you want a lot of the same things for your son—for him to be happy, feel good about himself, have friends, fit in, enjoy some favored activities. You probably disagree on how to help him get there, the role of sports in that, and where to draw the line for forcing the issue. Viewing it in terms of *she's too this/ he's not enough that* places the two of you at opposite corners of the ring. It becomes all one big unpleasant, unrelenting battle. When you add to that backdrop the goal of "getting" your wife to back off (introducing the near-impossible quest of making someone do something they don't want to do), you have all the ingredients for escalating standoffs, protracted power plays, and general ill humor around the house.

As an alternative, go to your wife and tell her you're worried the two of you are going to get stuck digging in ever deeper on your respective sides—that the more you feel she is protecting your son, the more you're probably going to feel the need to pull in the other direction, whether that means signing him up for more sports or exposing him to more risks associated with a sport. Does it make sense for the two of you to talk, *along with your son*, about all these things, and have him weigh in on how much and what type of involvement he wants from the two of you in relation to social or sports-related matters? Offer up something that you would be willing to do differently, or less intensively, and see if your wife will reciprocate with an offer of her own.

Helping Versus Enabling Your Nonathletic Son: Balancing Compassion and Support with Accountability

It sometimes is very hard for parents to find a good middle ground between not asking or expecting enough of their kids and asking or expecting too much. It's even harder when they know their child is struggling with some type of emotional problem or physical disability that makes learning and playing and maturing more challenging for him than it is for his peers. Feeling bad for their child, and wanting not to become an additional source of stress, they can be tempted to expect less of him than is healthy. Parents of children with social difficulties similarly may be tempted to make life within the family a little easier for their child wherever possible, figuring he has enough stress outside of it, during school and around the neighborhood.

Boys who don't like to play sports can sometimes fall into this category. The ones who have trouble locating friends or who get teased or excluded eventually bring those problems and the accompanying pain home with them, and the parents' handling of this can be an important influence on everything from how the boy learns to adapt to these challenges to how he and his siblings get along.

Harriet and Ron are the parents of twelve-year-old Scott. Scott loves making things like rockets and forts. His male peers have left rockets and forts behind in favor of video games and YouTube. Scott can't keep up with music, videos, or the middle school social scene, and as a result, the pack has left him behind.

"This has been the toughest year yet. It's like he's just not 'keeping up,' if you know what I mean," said Harriet. "I worry about him all the time."

Harriet had begun doing what a lot of parents do when they feel bad about what their children are going through: look the other way whenever their children do things they know they shouldn't be doing. Harriet didn't do this for Becky, though, Scott's sister. Whenever Becky acted sullen and nasty around the house, both her parents would jump on it immediately. "We'd just tell her that we don't go for that, and if she's got an issue, she either needs to tell us about it so that we can help her, or keep it to herself," replied Ron when I asked how he and his wife typically handled that type of situation. "We're not willing to be her punching bag for the evening when she's had a bad day."

But they handled it very differently when it came to Scott. "It's just that we feel so bad for him," Ron explained. "I mean he has so few friends, so if he comes home from school upset because some kid he asked over didn't want to come, I feel awful coming down on him for being in a bad mood. I'd be in one, too."

The problem, I explained to Scott's parents, wasn't Scott

being in a bad mood. It was the liberty he took of imposing his bad mood on others. And while it might be difficult for them to express their frustration with their son when they are also feeling sympathetic toward him, it would help all of them if they *found a way to express both sentiments separately*, even though they are experienced simultaneously.

"You can say to Scott," I suggested, "that you understand completely why he would be upset and that you don't expect him to just 'snap' out of his mood. But then tell him you don't want to continue to feel at the mercy of whether he has a good day or a bad day, and that you expect him to manage his emotions in a way that doesn't affect everyone in the household so strongly, just like you do with his sister."

Parents' concerns for their child's emotional welfare can create circumstances in which the child is given all kinds of "free passes" for personal and household responsibilities:

- He's having such a terrible year with all that's happened, so I'm just happy to see him make his way to school every day. I don't even bother to ask him about homework anymore.

- The last thing I want is for home life to become another source of stress. Who cares if he takes out the trash or not?

- With all the teasing my son gets at school for not being a jock-head, I frankly don't mind looking the other way if he gets a little pushy with his sister. She's teased him for years, and besides, she's tough. She can take it.

Well, maybe the sister can take it, but I'm not sure the brother-sister relationship will be able to. That's one of the unfortunate outcomes when parents hold one child way more accountable for his or her behavior than his or her siblings for long stretches of time, and justify it by saying that he or she is too stressed to have to deal with feeding the dog/being polite/having to wait his turn to get on the computer. This is different from giving a child some extra margin while he goes through a particularly bad period or deals with some specific personal problem. The extra support here, and its associated "bye," are time-limited expressions of kindness and consideration. Being able to treat their empathy for a son and their expectations of him as coexisting but separate feelings will help parents to avoid the tensions that can develop between siblings.

HELPING YOUR SON: THERE ARE OTHER THINGS BESIDES SPORTS

If the athletic or music or artistic community inside or outside of school is not a natural fit for your son, then dig around to find another one that is. You can help him find other kids who like raising Seeing Eye dogs or racing motorized go-karts or going downtown for sushi. There's chess, fencing, sailing, cooking, skeet shooting, beekeeping . . . the list goes on. Try something new together that neither of you would ever have expected to do: a murder-mystery club excursion, deep-sea fishing, or wakeboarding. Let your son know that he is not the only boy searching for something that can't be found on his school's menu of after-school activities.

Also consider humanitarian and community service opportunities. Some boys who aren't blessed with athletic talent are blessed with other traits that cause them to get teased when young but are valued highly by adults—sensitivity, introspection, and patience, for example. In the eyes of attentive parents and teachers and mentors, they can become standout citizens. "I have something to offer," was how twelve-year-old Logan explained his fondness for helping out at a community-funded senior center. Logan had a social anxiety disorder that prevented him from being able to talk comfortably with people he didn't know. It was easier for him to talk with the senior residents, who undoubtedly were less threatening than a group of his peers or his parents' friends. "I do better myself if I feel like I'm helping someone else," Logan reflected. "That way I'm not the only one having trouble doing something."

Creating Supportive Family Cultures for Boys Who Don't Care to Play Sports

Your home. It's one place where you have a decisive hand in determining what it feels like to be there. Parents will sometimes tell me they don't enjoy the atmosphere in their homes. *Someone's always mad at someone, or taking out their frustration on whoever's walking by,* they'll say. *There's too much yelling.*

Parents don't have to feel at the mercy of their children's unpleasant or unkind attitudes, and should feel empowered to say, *I don't like how it feels to live in this house right now. There's too much yelling and not enough support for one another and I want to change it.*

Some of that change can grow out of parents being attentive to the conversations and nonverbal communications exchanged among their kids as well as between themselves and their kids. Lecturing about respecting everyone in the household or trying harder to get along won't come close to doing the trick—they've heard it already, they know they're "supposed" to do that, or they think they already *are* doing it. And when they *don't* do it, it's because the other one started it, so they feel thoroughly justified.

Here's how it can happen more "organically."

They're a bunch of girls, Mom, a daughter says to her mother when asked if she and her friends were still planning on going to an outdoor event even though it is raining. *No one's going to want to go now that it's raining.*

Wow, that's an answer I wouldn't have expected in this day and age, her mom can say, leaving it at that. This is the kind of quickly interjected consciousness-raising remark that builds just enough of a foundation for the next time. Because maybe the next tossed-off remark on the part of this daughter will be something about how all real boys play sports or that all the really hot guys are built. The mother then piggybacks casually on her earlier comment, building some momentum to eventually, hopefully, culminate in a bit of self-awareness or insight on her daughter's part. *Wow, I wouldn't have expected that in this day and age, either . . .* Does the mother have to elaborate? No; the daughter knows what she means. And because it wasn't said as a way of pointed instruction but rather as part of an easy dialogue, the daughter is freer to become curious about her mom's response to her instead of angry and defensive.

Let's say you're in your kitchen, and this comment about "all real boys playing sports" comes from your own daughter, with your non-sports-playing son in the room. Here's a great opening for saying something, especially if you are able to present your point without apprehension or admonishment. *Nora, what's your brother supposed to do with that?* you could say. *He's right here. It's hard enough to battle the world on this issue. He shouldn't have to do it at home, too.*

Here's another example: You overhear one of your sons saying to another, *Why don't you ever want to do sports?* Don't leave it to them to work out; it'll end in a mess of bad feelings. Instead, consider this a beautiful opportunity to talk with them *together* about supporting each other even in the face of whatever great differences there are between them. Show them what the same question would look like if asked with compassion rather than with derision, and help the son who doesn't like sports come up with strong responses to his brother's question, which, inevitably, will be asked. It just should never again be asked by his brother.

Raising Boys to Be Good Sports

Given the wide margin boys get for behaving in a less than gracious manner when losing, it's not uncommon for parents to confuse poor sportsmanship with being competitive or even with being just a "normal" boy (as in, *Gee, I thought all boys get this way*). It's unfortunate, a lost opportunity for them to teach their kids that an appetite to win and good sportsmanship are not exclusive of each other.

Pay close attention to how your children conduct themselves in a variety of sports settings—from neighborhood pickup games to school practices to board games to impromptu thumb wrestles to races to be the first to get to the trampoline out back. Without being overbearing or too obvious, monitor your son's playing style and mood when he plays with other children. If he starts acting very competitive, or becomes glum or snappy or pushy, casually remind him that it's okay to want to win, as long as his opponent isn't made to feel bad in the process. Help him settle on a few decent expressions he can use for times he gets excited and wants to yell something out.

If you see your son getting overly excited or too aggressive, and you think he won't be able to take it down on his own, ask him and his friend to take a ten- or twenty-minute break. You can frame it in terms of things having gotten "pretty intense" and "it's probably a good time for a break." If your son resists, tell him privately, or at least very quietly, that until you feel he has better control over his playing behavior, you're going to take charge of situations you feel are not appropriate or that aren't fun for the other players. If he tells you you're overreacting, feel free to tell him that maybe you are, and that you'll think about it and discuss it with him later, but that for now you're going to insist on the short break. And then *follow that up* by going back to him later that day or the next about the question of whether you might be overreacting. Not doing that leaves your child thinking that you were just trying to get him to cooperate or, worse, hoping he'd forget. If your child's friend steps in and says, *No, it's okay, Mrs. B, he's kidding, we're fine . . .*, you can say, *Thanks, I appreciate you helping out, and, really, it may be no big deal at all, but I just want to let the air settle for a bit and then you guys can get right back to it. No worries.*

What if your son starts acting aggressively or poorly during a game at home with the family? Suspend the game for the moment and quietly but firmly stop him. Say, *That's not okay, Dan. Nobody wants to see you being miserable because the game isn't going your way.* Stopping the game action is important because it adds to the statement you're making, which is, *That type of behavior won't be tolerated anymore and I am willing to interrupt the game in order to stop it.* Often, parents tell me they do "something" along these lines. But as long as they are doing their "something" while everyone is still playing the game, it's not going to be as effective. For one thing, no one's really paying any attention to what the parent is saying, but more problematic is that it allows the acting-up child to stay (or feign being) absorbed in the activity, avoid making eye contact, and imply future compliance simply by not saying anything in defiance of what the parent has just said. The parent, relieved to not have been handed back an argument, is satisfied with the child's silent response, and cheerily returns to the game, only to have the drama repeat.

Stopping the game momentarily does something else helpful, too: *It makes the child feel a little self-conscious.* After all, game play has been held up so that he can be corrected. Everyone is looking, watching, waiting. In their heads, they're saying *C'mon, let's go,* and the child knows it. It's uncomfortable for him, a disincentive for repeating the objectionable behavior. But let's say soon afterward, your son does let fly with a rotten remark to little sister. Again, you stop the action, and have him immediately apologize. Then continue on as usual; the matter has been addressed and restitution made. The point never is to embarrass your son but to make the consequences of his choices regarding his game-playing behavior either disruptive or inconvenient enough to *him* that he decides the gratification he gets from his little digs just aren't worth it.

Families have varying comfort levels when it comes to competitiveness and displays of playful aggression, but most of us are on the same page when it comes to distinguishing between healthy swagger and bad sportsmanship. One is playful and the other is not. Shut down anything that sounds ugly or that wipes the smile off someone's face. That still leaves plenty of room for colorful (but nonaggressive) displays of overweening confidence, shameless conceit, and brazen trash talk to dress up Family Game Night.

HAVING BIG CONVERSATIONS ABOUT LITTLE THINGS

Ten-year-old Sam is telling you, his aunt, about his upcoming birthday party. Sam loves sports, and is planning to fill the day with them. He says something about a new friend who's coming, adding, "I don't know what he's going to do all day because he doesn't play any sports. But I guess that's his problem."

INEFFECTIVE RESPONSES:

Sam, don't say that. It's not very nice.

Well, why did you invite him then if you don't think he'll have a good time?

Oh, great, now what are we supposed to do?

BETTER ALTERNATIVES:

That's great you invited him—what everyone wants is to be included. I'm proud of you. So how do we make sure everyone has fun? Nobody feels good as an outsider.

OR:

You: Why do you say it's his problem? Wouldn't you feel at least a little responsible for making sure he has a good time?

Sam: Well, it's my birthday party.

You: Yeah, it is, but you make it sound as if it's all about you. It's about you and your guests, and he's your guest.

Sam: Well, what am I supposed to do, make him play sports that day?

You: C'mon, don't get defensive. There was a reason you invited him and it probably had nothing to do with whether or not he played sports. You probably are used to having a good time together doing something else. Don't bail on him now.

Sam: So what am I supposed to do?

You: I don't know, I don't have a perfect answer, I guess just being sensitive to the situation is a good place to start. Put yourself in his shoes. Maybe play a couple of things you know he likes to do or might join in with. And if he doesn't, then just talk to him during breaks and stuff, so he doesn't feel totally left out. Those few things could make a huge difference for him.

CHAPTER NINE

Whenever Anyone Loses, Everyone Loses

Among all the issues covered in this book, perhaps the most central one is this: that once any community—social, ethnic, religious, national, or global—begins to accept or even tolerate the marginalization of one part of its constituency while another is idealized, *everyone* in that community begins losing something.

We already know how boys who don't match up closely with our nation's masculine ideals are disadvantaged. Sometimes we lose some of those boys: The depression, isolation, ingrained bitterness, or loss of self-confidence that can come from feeling like a second-class citizen gradually robs them of their generosity, benevolence, trust, or positive spirit, denying us the best they would have had to

> **"Injustice anywhere is a threat to justice everywhere."**
>
> Reverend Martin Luther King Jr.

offer; with suicide, of course, we're denied them altogether, forever. Parents, too, suffer, to greater or lesser degrees, burdened by the worry, frustration, chronic conflict, or the haunting helplessness that comes from having to witness your own child in pain.

And, despite ours still being a patriarchal culture, it's no stroll in the park for the other guys either. "Manhood is the leaden mythology riding on the shoulders of every man," concluded Norah Vincent after her year of living disguised as a man. In her book *Self-Made Man: One Woman's Journey into Manhood and Back Again,* which we first mentioned in Chapter Six, Vincent describes her experience as "ungainly, suffocating, torpor-inducing" because of what she found to be men's indelible need to hide their real selves from the world. It looks like even the bullies crash at some point, their moments of seeming triumph becoming more hollow over time before altogether revealing each one's alienating, ugly underside.

In one way or another, really, every one of us is affected when institutions and customs and our selective attention allow injustices to be casually perpetuated. Even the composite character of our nation, and the face it wears, bear the stamp of America's unfaltering allegiance to traditional masculine ideals. On more than a few occasions America has been criticized by the international community, as well as by its own citizens, for its aggressive and domineering comportment on the global stage. In addition, America's strong ideological allegiances to some of its founding principles—independence, pioneerism, and fortitude—appear to serve as justification for coming off as aloof and self-righteous.

When advanced with hubris, it all can start looking a lot like the self-rule and zeal of a playground bully.

Our nation's slim definitions of masculinity and its endorsement of boys' more aggressive features cost us in another way, too. The self-induced myopia puts us at risk for overlooking the collective and individual voices of boys who are silenced by their marginalization, and who could otherwise offer a variety of nontraditional male perspectives. *Manliness* author Harvey C. Mansfield alluded to this in his 2006 interview with Peter W. Schramm, executive director of the John M. Ashbrook Center for Public Affairs at Ashland University, by criticizing the intolerant manly man for "failing to see the need for poets and thinkers and other people who aren't men of action."[1]

I don't share Mansfield's definition of poets and thinkers as people who aren't men of action and do, personally, conceptualize activity as including the kind we can't see or hear—thinking, writing, composing, constructing, theorizing, and observing come to mind. I suppose Mansfield's men of action are the "doers" in our society—teachers and loggers and physicians and masons. I think of poets and thinkers as men of action, too, only that their activity takes place internally or privately or quietly, but no less significantly. I also think that the actions of these men who are not "men of action" (i.e., journalists, playwrights, musicians, scientists, sculptors) can have terrifically profound and widespread effects not only on the people with whom they are in direct contact (their audiences, readerships, students) but on the families and communities and institutions within which these people live and work, something akin to second-order change. That's a lot of activity.

Take someone like American composer, conductor, and master teacher Leonard Bernstein, for example. A peerless intellectual and creative force in the world of music and theater until his death in 1990, Bernstein gave us gifts that made the world a little smaller and us a little bigger. This was a man who deeply understood the power of sound, and saw it as an unassailable weapon in the war against the barbarities that come from human prejudice and intolerance and hate for those unlike oneself: "This will be our reply to violence: to make music more intensely, more beautifully, and more devotedly than before."

It's a demonstration of the belief that pens can sometimes be mightier than swords, or at least offer a different vision of how peace could come about. Perhaps one of the many reasons for Bernstein's enduring legacy is that through the evocative power of his many compositions, the people in his audiences were able to see that, too. Bernstein taught us that music held a power compelling enough to be counted among our greatest natural forces.

I've Never Met a Happy Bully

Most bullies haven't any idea how compromised they are by their attraction to the act of exploiting other human beings. Exerting that kind of pain without recoiling at their own actions requires them to have detached emotionally from the victim's feelings as well as their own, and it's a slippery slope from there. They start losing the freedom to see people for who they truly are and, in the saddest of cases, live lonely lives in distorted, black-and-white worlds in which inhabitants are either winners or losers—a moral reduction of the grossest sort, serving to make their environments less ambiguous and therefore more controllable, but totally bereft of any sort of real companionship.

There are other kinds of bullies, too. They step into the role out of a need to protect their picture of who they are, or avoid a painful truth about someone else, or deflect problems elsewhere. Some of the teenagers I see in my practice are like this; they aren't by nature opportunistic, and don't enjoy having to hurt or push away someone else in order to shield themselves. But they're stuck, and their parents are stuck, and their reactions to each other keep pushing them deeper into the conflict. For instance, I am increasingly brought adolescents who, in the throes or wake of depression or anxiety or loss, have been allowed to take over the household by moms and/or dads reluctant to impose any type of limit they feel could potentially cause the teen more stress. And so the adolescent, sensing at some level an opportunity to exploit the parents' anxiety about "making things worse," becomes more demanding, and the parents more accommodating, and the cycle perpetuates itself. The bully materializes, gets fed, and grows a little meaner.

Fourteen-year-old Nina was brought in for therapy by her war-weary mom. "She's angry and depressed all the time and she takes it out on me," Nina's mother explained. "I try to help her but she just throws it back in my face and tells me that if I really wanted to help her I'd let her do whatever she wants whenever she wants. I don't, obviously, but sometimes I feel so bad for her and how she feels that I find myself actually thinking about it."

I watched the dynamic between this mother and daughter unfold. The mother would try to get Nina to talk, and Nina would respond minimally—one word, two words, no words. Mom would try again. Nina became annoyed. The more annoyed Nina became with her mother's attempts to get her to participate, the more tentative the mother's attempts became. Moreover, the more urgent Nina's mother's tone became while she described her daughter's problems to me, the more indifferent Nina became. At one point, Nina interrupted her mother's account of a recent night when, at Nina's hysterical request, she'd spent the night in her daughter's room, consoling her and calming her down until the wee hours of the morning. Nina only wanted to know where they were going to eat after the session. Now it was my turn to interrupt.

"Is your daughter always this dismissive of your attempts to help her?"

"Yes," came the mother's emphatic response, looking at her daughter. "I've never known anyone who could make me feel so stupid for simply caring about her."

This dynamic rarely self-corrects. However, with intervention, it can be altered pretty quickly. In Nina's case, I suggested to her mother (with Nina there) that when the opportunity presented itself, she say to her daughter something along the following lines: *I love you so very much, and feel very badly that you're not happy, and would do anything in this world for you. But I've realized that because I have been so worried about you and feel so bad about it, I've pretty much been letting you do as you please. I stopped asking you to help around the house. I stopped asking you to stop moping or cursing. I've stopped expecting you to get all your assignments in on time. I've even stopped expecting you to treat me respectfully, and it's been a disservice to both of us. So, while I'll help you with whatever it is you're going through, I'm not going to let my feeling bad for you, or my anxiety about "making things worse" between us, get in the way of my setting limits where they're needed.*

I said to Nina's mother in this same session that I thought her daughter's mistreatment of her and her depression were probably related. I said that I didn't believe any kid who allowed herself to treat a loved one that way really could feel good about herself or about their relationship. And that by silencing her mother in order to prop up her self-esteem and hide from painful emotions or problems, Nina was only digging a deeper hole for herself and free-falling into a deeper depression. I told them both that Nina *needed her mom to say that it bothered her* when Nina discounted her efforts to help her, and that it was unacceptable. I imagined that at least some of Nina's problems stemmed from her trying to relate this way with others—friends, classmates, teachers, and relatives—people who were going to be less tolerant than her parents were of her moodiness and disrespect. Trying to "get" Nina to talk about herself and her feelings—a common but often ill-applied therapeutic strategy with adolescents—would only have resulted in a kid who felt questioned to death and resentful of a process that disregarded her message (*I don't want to talk about it*), and a mom who would still be responding to her daughter in the same unproductive way. I've found that once parents change how they relate to their children with regard to prominent family issues, the door is open for the children to come forward more candidly about their problems. Some of these kids then go on to ask, very maturely and directly, for more help, which is exactly what Nina did within a few weeks of this first meeting.

We could use this same model of intervention to help parents who are aware of their kids' aggressive behavior toward other kids, but uncertain about how to intervene because of wanting, at the same time, to be sensitive to their child's own pain or struggles. This is what was happening to Donna, Jared's mother. "All that happens is that I end up yelling at him to stop, and then he tears up, and I tear up and just feel worse," says Donna, describing her typical reaction to Jared's physical aggressiveness toward his younger brother. Eleven years old and not by nature an aggressive child, Jared was frequently teased at school for being poor at sports, as well as for having taken up the cello. "I know why he does it," Donna explained. "He spends six hours every day either putting up with all kinds of crap at school because he happens to dislike soccer and like the cello, or avoiding kids so that he won't be teased, and by the time he gets home he's a mess. So he takes it out on his little brother, who puts up with it because he likes to act like a little macho man himself, especially to his big brother. Jared's days are already so frustrating for him that I feel bad getting on his case and adding to it even more, or punishing him. It just feels wrong."

I began explaining to Donna how her sympathy for Jared was

influencing her responses to his misbehavior, and inadvertently teaching him that it's acceptable to pass your anger down the line. I also told Donna that she had a lot of options besides punishing Jared, and that in fact I thought a more effective consequence, regardless of how bad Jared's day was at school, was to ask him to make some sort of restitution to his brother anytime he hurt him. This could be anything from doing a few of his brother's chores, to cooking his brother a meal, to simply writing a letter of apology. This would force Jared to be accountable directly to his brother, very possibly a stronger disincentive than having to skip a night of television.

Another mom, overwhelmed with the challenge of managing the aggressive, bullying behavior of her fourteen-year-old son toward his nonathletic younger brother, would intervene only when things got way out of hand. Over time, her late arrival on these scenes allowed this older brother to wear the cloak of aggression more and more comfortably, and more brazenly. I worried that he himself was also becoming more comfortable with his intolerance for others not like himself. I suggested to the mother that instead of waiting to see if the boys worked it out themselves, which they never did anyway, she impose a zero-tolerance rule for any aggression or violence whatsoever: no name-calling, dissing, shoving, mean jokes, offensive gestures, or teasing. Her response? "You've got to be kidding! I'll be doing nothing but monitoring the two boys!" And mine was, "Yes, you are going to be grossly and ridiculously inconvenienced in the beginning, but they at least will be inconveniences of your choosing. Second, you'll be showing your boys that you really mean what you say because they'll see what you're willing to deal with in order to follow through. And third, once they understand that you will interrupt all their shenanigans, all the time, it will start to become so darn annoying they'll more than likely just drop it."

The Lonely Witness

No one feels good in an environment in which only some people are safe. The more arbitrary the criteria for being excluded, the more anxiety is created in those who are worried they could be next. For this as well as other reasons, studies are showing that students who witness acts of bullying are likely to report even greater psychological distress than either the students who were doing the bullying or the ones who were actually bullied.[2] Another source of this extra distress seems to be the guilt felt for not intervening, or worse, *from vacillating* between doing what they thought they should do (i.e., help the victim) and not acting for fear of then being victimized themselves.

Historically, many antibullying programs have focused on the excluder (bully) and the excluded (bullied). More recently, they have broadened the focus to include help for kids witnessing the activity as well. Studies conducted in Finland and in Canada show that most instances of bullying are actually witnessed by peers.[3] And while these young witnesses surely need our support, too, they also could wind up being a valuable resource in our battles against bullying. School assemblies make countless efforts to address these issues, but much of the information and educational opportunities are lost on large groups of fidgeting children or distracted teens. But what if instead we worked with kids in small-group formats, focusing on schoolwide team building and on identifying leaders within the student body who can be instrumental in changing the social climate inside of their school. For instance, these leaders could work toward cultivating social cultures at their respective schools that naturally inhibit bullying behavior *by purposely not rewarding it* (for example, kids would be primed to resist smiling or looking at the victim, and instead stare at the perpetrator) or *by standing next to the victim(s)* in quiet support. These students would know ahead of time which other students would be willing to act, too, so that no one has to act alone. Kids who do intervene in these kinds of situations, either directly with the bully or by informing an adult, have in fact been found to have a higher social status in general,[4] something which can be capitalized upon in order to galvanize groups of students, as well as take some of the power away from the bully and redistribute among witnesses.

RAISING AWARENESS ABOUT THE NEGATIVE IMPACT ON CHILDREN WHO WITNESS BULLYING, AND CAPITALIZING ON THEIR POTENTIAL TO LEAD CHANGE

Get discussions rolling between yourself and your children, or among a bunch of kids, that address very honestly what it's like to actually witness kids being teased or excluded.

We often "talk" about these types of life experiences by simply lecturing about the "importance of speaking up for others" and other clichés. Talks that "stick" are the ones that kids feel are relevant to their lives because they touch upon the specific social or personal questions that rise up for them under those circumstances. Even better, talk about your own experiences having been party to or having witnessed unkind treatment from one or more kids to another, and what your reaction to it was. Mention in particular any situation where you didn't know what to do, felt caught in the middle, knew you were letting someone down by not intervening, or maybe even secretly enjoyed seeing the kid being teased. Help kids to understand that sometimes we have more than one feeling at the same time, and that witnessing behavior you find offensive can bring this out. Explain how for some situations there are no good solutions, just different choices to be made, each one carrying its own set of pluses and minuses.

While visiting the UN ambassador from Kenya in New York, Stanford University premed student Wilson Kimeli Naiyomah witnessed the terrorist attacks on the World Trade Center. A Maasai warrior from the Kenyan village of Enoosaen, a village composed mostly of mud huts, Kimeli urgently felt a need to do something to help the situation, but didn't know what that could be. He told his fellow villagers about the attacks, explaining that the buildings targeted were so tall that, from their windows, people jumped to their deaths. Deeply saddened and troubled by this account, the villagers of Enoosaen decided, Kimeli explained, to give "the gift of solace": fourteen head of cattle, the Maasai's most prized possession and precious gift. Tribal elders presented the cows to the acting American ambassador at a formal ceremony attended by hundreds of Maasai holding banners, some of which read, "To the people of America, we give these cows to help you."[5]

This story was cited by Harvard Medical School psychology professor and founding director of the Witnessing Project, Kaethe Weingarten, and the resonance of the pain felt by the Maasai villagers and their gifting of the cattle is an example of what she calls "compassionate witnessing." Rooted in this response is a recognition and an expression of our common bond with one another—not because we necessarily *identify* with the other, but because of a kinship that allows us to be moved by the experience of another human being whose psychological constitution, daily tasks of living, and/or cultural and ethical values might be disorientingly different from our own. Weingarten noted that the impact of the Maasai's acknowledgment of American suffering and sorrow was significant, evoking a reciprocal appreciation, initiating a remarkable process of connection, and serving as both a symbolic and literal act of humanity that was understood all over the world.

People often say they find it easier to empathize with individuals with whom they share a history or religion or culture or occupation than with individuals with whom they feel they have little in common. At first blush it makes sense; you figure you can more easily appreciate what someone else is going through once you've "been there" or at least know a bunch of other people who have been there. At the very least, you are familiar with some of the circumstances. But by complacently accepting this idea that, in order to understand other people, you have to walk a mile in their shoes, we've trained ourselves *not* to expect to easily understand or empathize with somebody who is different from us. And so, following the path of any other self-fulfilling prophecy, we find ourselves needlessly flummoxed or uncomprehending or impassive in the face of a stranger's pain.

In one of my favorite stories from graduate school, a client asks her therapist how he would ever be able to understand her grief over losing her husband if he hadn't gone through a similar experience. And he replied softly with, "I don't have to be seven feet tall in order to know what it feels like to be self-conscious in public."[6] We all have experiences we can use to help bridge the gap between what others tell us and what we understand. Compassionate witnessing aids us in recognizing our shared humanity and restoring it when it falters. It might also be one of the best vehicles the global community has for thwarting the pernicious process of dehumanization that makes it so easy for too many to decide others' fates.

In the 2010 film *Biutiful,* Javier Bardem plays the role of Uxbal, a Barcelona black marketer who traffics in illegal workers. He has two children whom he loves deeply and an ex-wife who badly abuses drugs and alcohol. Bardem's character has been diagnosed with inoperable cancer, and he is trying to put his life in order before his impending death. Interviewed about his role in the film, Bardem spoke about how affected he was by its difficult material, and how he balanced its poignant draw into the lives of endangered, desperate people for whom he felt great compassion, with the need to respectfully recognize the limits of his power to change their living conditions.

"We live in a world where everything [is] theoretical," Bardem says during his interview, "everything is witnessed from a distance. It's in the Internet, it's in the newspapers, it's in the news. But when it comes this close to you, there's no way you can protect [yourself] through cynicism . . . It doesn't mean save the world, it means just like be aware of that, and be responsible for that, and your own actions." Witnessing like this offers us opportunities not only to affect the *other*, in the way the Maasai affected a shell-shocked America, but opportunities to affect ourselves, if we let it, as Bardem did in the process of preparing for his role.

". . . But when you approach the real life of those people," adds Bardem, referring to having visited undocumented foreigners living under despairing conditions in Barcelona, " . . . they are not numbers anymore, or ghosts . . . you see yourself in all of them, saying I could be that one, or that one, or that one. And then the experience becomes emotional and physical, rather than just a theoretical experience . . ."[7]

One Voice Can Matter

On August 20, 1971, a psychology professor at Stanford University by the name of Philip Zimbardo led a team of researchers in what came to be known as the Stanford Prison Experiments, a study of the psychological effects of being a prisoner or prison guard. Zimbardo's interest in conducting the experiment had been in examining the power of roles, rules, symbols, group identity, and the situational validation of behavior that would ordinarily repulse people exposed to it. Through his earlier research studies on deindividuation, vandalism, and dehumanization, Zimbardo was able to demonstrate the ease with which ordinary people could be led to engage in antisocial acts by putting them in situations in which they either felt anonymous, or could somehow perceive others as being less than human.

Though scheduled to last two weeks, the experiment was stopped five days after it began as a result of the horrific and unexpected abuse suffered by the "prisoners" (college students) at the hands of the "prison guards" (also college students). The experiment even affected Zimbardo himself, who, in his capacity as "Prison Superintendant," lost sight of his role as psychologist and permitted the abuse to continue as though it were a real prison. It was aborted only when graduate student Christina Maslach, intending to conduct interviews with these students, was introduced to the experiment and vehemently objected to the appalling conditions of the prison. *Fifty* outside observers had already come and gone before Maslach questioned the ethics of Zimbardo's experiment, bringing it to a screeching halt. "She challenged us to examine the madness she observed, that we had created and had to take responsibility for," said Zimbardo at a 1996 Toronto symposium.[8]

We have as much responsibility to teach our children about speaking up when things aren't right as we do to speak up ourselves, no matter how few are affected. My dear friend Andrea Lovett once shared with me this story: A storm leaves thousands of starfish washed up on the shore. The next day they're all drying up in the sun, and a woman comes to toss them back into the ocean. A passerby stops and says, "Why are you bothering? It's not going to matter—there are thousands of them." And throwing another starfish into the water, the woman turns to the passerby and replies, "Well, it mattered to that one."

CHAPTER TEN

Becoming Effective Agents of Change

We shouldn't feel at the mercy of all the different forces shaping our children's social milieu any more than we should believe we are in control of them. But somewhere between those two extremes lies an abundance of opportunities for changing the ways in which nonnormative boys and girls are regarded and treated. With the hopeful but daunting task of instigating changes across many settings, we begin, like any good general of warfare, by studying the enemy.

This enemy resides in our history as well as in our pop culture, and wears one face as global as gender socialization, and another as familiar as the boy next door. We have, for example, gender norms that tell us what boys should like to play and how they should move and talk and relate to each other. We have family traditions and expectations about raising sons, and parent anxieties about having a boy who is anything but adroit on the playground. We have a vast, inescapable, sticky web of electronic entertainment networks bombarding kids with in-your-face images and character heroes who champion cavalier attitudes about everything from physical aggression to social manipulation to the disposability of human beings. We have competitive drives from our own human nature that need tempering and social dynamics between people that need to be modified and a lot of stereotyping and mythmaking about boys being kinesis personified. And we can't forget the hungry youth sports industry present in just about every American community, ready to harvest the next crop of four- and five-year-olds, and the school subculture that, for some boys, is nothing but a wolf in sheep's clothing.

> "We teach in the deepest way—by example."
>
> Lawrence LeShan, *The Dilemma of Psychology*

The bias against boys who don't enjoy playing sports is almost everywhere. That's a lot of places, but it's also a lot of opportunity to change things around.

Shaping Social Contexts to Influence Social Ordering

Put a group of people together for long enough and the jockeying for position will begin; we are hardwired to impose order in ambiguous situations. Social dominance—this instinct for social ordering that scientists tell us is intrinsic to the human race—always puts some of us on top, some of us in the middle, and some of us on the bottom. This book being about boys, and with social context driving group values, it's pretty obvious which children are going to occupy the top and bottom rungs. Kids stick pretty close to the rules they know.

We can't stop social ordering from taking place, but by orchestrating some of the contexts in which it happens, we can sometimes affect its outcome. For instance, Richard Louv, first mentioned in Chapter Two and author of *Last Child in the Woods: Saving Our Children from Nature-Deficit Disorder*, has taught us that putting children in natural settings to play has the potential to alter social hierarchies because the social economics of the group change in such environments. All of a sudden the physical skills that served boys so well on the playground take a backseat to the imaginative, creative, and language skills that can elevate playing in the woods to a near art form. Louv has also taught us that the rise over the past thirty years in public funding for sports over parks, as well as in the number of for-profit indoor play centers, has meant that more and more children are now playing in structured play settings where athletically adept kids are destined to shine. Putting kids in natural play settings will be a lot easier once we find ways to modify or at least match the growth of sports centers and structured parks with better access to small forests and shallow streams and ungroomed fields. Then the hard part comes: getting kids to go in them.

> Change the context in which social ordering takes
> place in order to affect a different outcome.

Can we cultivate other settings where skills or traits beside athleticism or ruggedness are useful and might be valued by the larger peer group? Schools seem an obvious choice, though it will be an uphill climb—through no fault of administration. For the most part, the social climates of schools, taken as heterogeneous communities, are largely influenced by the most visible, audible, and socially powerful subset of students—and guess who that is. Teachers innocently play into this, too. They wear school colors on game days and dress their classrooms with banners of their favorite pro teams. It's benign and malignant at the same time; cheering your teams on is compelling, but the communal roar does block out the school's other sounds.

Some schools have managed to shape a more democratic student body. "At my school, the kids who play sports and the kids who are into drama or in National Honor Society all get along really well," a fifteen-year-old therapy client of mine once said. "It's like everyone respects what everyone else is into. I think the reason why we get along is that we all have in common that we're smart, and we kind of like that." Heidi's school was a small charter high school in a metropolitan suburb, with a mission blurb that talks about empowering students to recognize their own uniqueness and talent while instilling critical thinking skills, a respect for diversity, and an appreciation of scholarship and responsibility. It reads well, sure, but they're actually getting it to work.

It's unrealistic and contrived for schools to consider downplaying their enthusiasm for athletics only so that other activities and the kids who participate in them can get noticed. Some things are just louder than others. But we could ask schools to amp up those other activities, or at least amp up their visibility within the school community.

> Schools can make a point to showcase the accomplishments and talents of students who are doing interesting things not on the playing fields and courts but in the community or in their own homes.

Schools can balance out the recognition of students' sports-related accomplishments with non-sports-related accomplishments in several ways. For instance, most schools have committees in place to make sure that pep rallies and Spirit Days are properly promoted and that morning announcements include all the athletic victories from the prior day. Why not start a committee to gather and report news about the talents and/or recent contributions of student writers, artists, linguists, budding business leaders, animal trainers, social activists, community service volunteers, musicians, and caretakers of the elderly, ailing parents, or siblings? Taking it a step further, what about school administrators allowing a student's committed extracurricular participation in music, theater, or art substitute for credit-bearing athletic activities offered by the school? After all, it's not unheard of for students to get phys ed credit for their elite-level involvement in nationally and internationally competitive sports such as horseback riding and figure skating.

Some boys who don't play sports and tend also to hang back in demanding social situations will just shine around animals. Schools might consider adding some of following (off-the-beaten-path) afterschool activities as *group* community service opportunities: volunteering at wildlife rescue centers; helping to train dogs for service, obedience, and rescue work; and volunteering at therapeutic horseback-riding centers that work with disabled children. Not only will these opportunities serve as ways for these boys to meet like-minded kids, participating in them will help them build a stronger connection to their school—something that kids who aren't active in sports or conventional after-school clubs often miss out on. To boot, any one of them would make a terrific senior project. Many schools have developed exit projects for seniors that reflect active citizenship. These types of projects explore various issues affecting the community, and students are required to research and develop strategies to address the resulting problems. Some of them even come up with pilot projects. One such project could be highlighting the challenges faced by nonathletic boys in a particular community and the artificial power harnessed by the athletic subcommunity or by bullies or other identifiable social groups.

Disabling the Bully's Power

There is a huge difference between the natural social ordering that takes place silently and swiftly among children, and bullying. Most people have an innate sense of where they belong on the scales of popularity and power, and generally accept their placement if it's felt to be legitimate—that is, neither political nor vengeful. What they can't accept, and shouldn't, is being hammered for landing on the lower rungs by the very ones who placed them there.

Kids tease and boss around other kids in order to gain a sense of control, appear to be the head honcho, discharge frustration, fit in with a certain crowd, look tough, impress peers, or scare prospective bullies off. For certain kids, being mean to someone sometimes just feels good. This is the darker side of that social-ordering instinct, a dimension of humanity that was ever so tragically and graphically demonstrated, as mentioned earlier, in William Golding's classic novel *Lord of the Flies*—as was its twin, the civilizing instinct we all carry as well. On Golding's isolated tropical island, where a dozen or so English schoolboys survive a plane crash and are forced to create their own makeshift version of civilization, the conflicting forces of savagery and civility, nestled in the instincts of each of these boys, compete for dominance and leave in their wake a catastrophic reminder of what humans are capable of doing to one another.

Stop the cycle of aggression in which boys escape
being bullied by finding victims of their own.

Today, however, the stage upon which these competing instincts play out is the more civilized venue of the schoolyard or neighborhood haunt, and matters of life or death give way to less literal meanings of survival—regard among peers, freedom from bullying, safety from exclusionary practices. Nonetheless, power is power is power.

Some kids wind up picking on others because it's the only way they know how to get a bully off their own back. "I picked out another boy, someone worse off than me . . ." explained a high school student, tearfully recounting his torment in middle school and his method for finally stopping it. In a study about normative and marginalized masculinities, fifteen-year-old Billy, who described himself as a "nerd and teacher's pet" in second through fifth grade, explained how with his entry into middle school, he recovered a level of popularity he'd last held in first grade:

"I went to a school with a very big fighting emphasis . . . And I wasn't really into fighting. But EVERYBODY was being mean to me. And so . . . I just up and beat someone up. And then all of a sudden everybody . . . liked me. Cuz that's just what you have to do to earn their respect." [1]

STOPPING THE CYCLE OF AGGRESSION

IN SCHOOLS:

Talk about the pressure kids feel to shake off being teased or excluded by perpetrating the abuse on someone else. Wonder out loud about the kind of moral dilemma this might be for some kids who abhor violence and don't want to fight but feel that their choice is taking someone down or being taken down. Find kids who are willing to volunteer to tell their stories about this dilemma, including some who succumbed to the pressure, and what kind of effect it had on them. Looking back, how would they have preferred to handle it? How could teachers or school officials have helped? What would they do now that they didn't know to do then? What advice do they have for kids who are in a similar situation? Would they be willing to be available to kids who want to talk about their own struggles with these matters in a confidential setting?

AT HOME:

Ask your son if he has ever felt the need to bully or tease somebody as a way of getting kids to leave *him* alone? You can start by normalizing the behavior—not as something that's okay, but as something that happens. Let him know up front that you're not trying to "trick" him into telling you something you'll later be angry about. Explain that you're trying to help him figure out how to be the guy he truly is rather than the guy the other kids think he's "supposed" to be. Share with him any stories from your own childhood that have to do with either bullying or being bullied for seeming different from the other boys. If you did a lot of bullying, or were the leader in making other kids feel excluded from a group, talk about how you evolved from a person who thought it was funny or cool to get another kid to cry or get mad, to the person you are now.

Social dynamics whose rules are unspoken but communally acknowledged thrive in clandestine climates and quickly wilt when examined in the light of day. Let's take, for example, girl bullying, in which one girl is disingenuously complimenting another, less popular girl. The success of the act—in this case the public humiliation of an unsuspecting party—is dependent upon the reluctance of anyone to call the bully out on the duplicitous nature of her interaction with the target. Anyone who sees what's happening knows exactly what's going on, but reacts outwardly only to the face value of the act, not its intention.

By *making more explicit* the covert dynamics behind certain bullying behaviors, we interfere with the integrity of these (public) acts. One way of doing this is to closely examine the acts under the communal microscope known as a school's student body. Get kids talking in the classroom about how people who have intentions of playing with their classmates' feelings count on witnesses to stay out of it. Talk with them about all the ways in which this kind of bully works at guaranteeing that level of collusion, such as exploiting her popularity or her power, or threatening dissenters with their own exclusion from the group. When, as a part of talking with would-be witnesses to bullying, we break down and pick apart all the unspoken codes and social rules dictating how they are supposed to respond in its presence, we make it harder in the future for them to feign naïveté, believe they're the only bystander who recognizes the bullying for what it is, or remain silent. Moreover, it changes things for the bully as well, who, having been part of these group discussions— incognito, of course—cannot "do her thing" without wondering if others, too, are aware that she is doing it. In the end, it can never quite roll out the same way again.

Disempower the unspoken, covert dynamics behind bullying by making them explicit.

Self-consciousness—that awareness of oneself in the moment that can be anything from mildly uncomfortable to paralyzing— is typically thought of as one of those unavoidable by-products of the human experience. It's the price we pay for being able to recognize ourselves in action, and when used sensitively, it can be an exquisitely effective means of influencing kids to change— especially those who reject our more direct requests.

A mother of a teenage daughter asked me what she could do about her daughter's disrespectful tone of voice and manner of speaking to her at home. She said it always got worse when her daughter's friends were around. The mother had tried talking to her daughter about it, and had even taken away her cell phone a few times, all to no avail. Her daughter would simply flip her hair through the air and act as if she hadn't been planning to use the phone for a while anyway.

I suggested to the mother that the next time her daughter talked to her disrespectfully in front of her friends, she should simply stop whatever she was doing and look at her daughter. In the past, not wanting to embarrass her daughter, the mother would ignore her, or try to make a joke of what she'd said, as if they were all just kidding, or walk off with a slow burn. I directed the mother to not say anything, and just wait. The abrupt halting of action on her part, and her visual focus on her daughter, *the track of which would be followed by the friends in the room,* would very suddenly and unexpectedly *put the attention on the daughter* instead of—as the daughter was expecting—on the embarrassed mother. Kids don't like it when their attempts to control the social environment leave them in the spotlight instead of the person they'd intended it for.

> Allow the natural human aversion to feeling
> self-conscious help us in our efforts to shape
> unbecoming behavior while avoiding
> protracted power struggles.

I explained to the mother that by stopping, and looking, everything that needed to be said was said, albeit nonverbally: that what her daughter had said was unacceptable; that she was no longer going to pretend it didn't affect her or she didn't hear it; that anytime her daughter took the liberty of speaking to her like that she should expect to have to account for it, no matter who was present; and that she—the mom—was no longer going to allow herself to worry more about her daughter feeling embarrassed in front of friends than her daughter was going to worry.

This is the elegance of using self-consciousness to influence a person's choice of actions. The mother was able to intervene in her daughter's inappropriate behavior without inciting an argument or giving the daughter more ammunition for her defiance. There is nothing for the daughter to fight. When her mother stops and looks over at her, as if to say, *Wow, I can't believe you just said that*, the daughter can only stand there and make some attempt at dismissing her mother's stance as ridiculous in some way—which in all likelihood would come off as lame and pathetic to her friends—or change the topic quickly and pretend that nothing happened.

> Make support for antibullying in schools visible, omnipresent, and appealing to its intended audience. That means no more middle and high school antibullying posters using cartoon characters in primary colors.

Schools can strengthen their stand against bigotry and bullying by providing tangible evidence that such a stand exists. Most important is making the evidence something kids will find appealing. Authorize students to go online and locate organizations such as Musicians Opposed to Bullying or Entertainers

Against Bullying from which they can purchase posters. Put them up *everywhere:* in the bathroom stalls, on the seat backs of school buses, in classrooms, on the walls in desolate corners of school. Invite kids to form a "news watch," where they have permission to track down antibullying songs from artists such as Rise Against or Eminem and Lil Wayne that can be played over the PA system in the morning before classes start. Using media that will hold kids' attention, teachers can show antibullying videos from these same artists as a way to prompt discussions about bullying and empathy and bystander effects. A lot of students will already have seen these videos. Why do they watch them, "on their own time," so to speak? Does anything about the antibullying message make them think about that problem, or are they really only interested in the music? If they were making their own antibullying video, what kind of story line would they use? Whose music would they include? How would the video end? Would they maybe want to actually make one?

More tangible evidence of a school's stand against bullying, discrimination, and exclusionary social practices can come in the form of voluntary antibullying brigades—kids who wear their intolerance for cruelty on their sleeves, either literally, as in a pin or patch, or figuratively, in their willingness to stand out and do something about the problem. These students would be charged with keeping their eyes peeled for surreptitious activity in hallways, lunchrooms, buses, locker rooms, and courtyards and intervening peacefully with perhaps nothing more than their presence. They can also receive some basic training in defusing aggressive verbal escalations and the "friendly" trash talk that, much like forest flash fires, rapidly get out of control.

> **Start student-led antibullying brigades in schools. Help kids become stakeholders in the quality of the social climates in which they spend six hours every day.**

Babies. Go figure. Instead of us getting *tougher* with bullies, recent research studies are showing that you can impact them more by going softer—as in, by using babies. Seems that around babies, tough kids smile, disruptive kids focus, and shy kids open up. That's what Mary Gordon and her Toronto-based Roots of Empathy program have discovered.

Roots of Empathy is a classroom program showing great results reducing levels of aggression among schoolchildren while also enhancing their social/emotional competence and empathic capabilities. At the heart of the program are neighborhood parents who, along with their infants, make monthly visits to a specific classroom over the school year. Guided by Roots instructors, the kids in the classroom not only observe the baby and the relationship between baby and parent, but are enlisted to do things to care for the baby, such as singing songs or speaking gently to the baby.

The results, apparently, can be dramatic. One study of first- to third-grade classrooms focused on the subset of kids who exhibited "proactive aggression"—the deliberate and cold-blooded aggression of bullies who prey on vulnerable kids. Of those who participated in the Roots program, 88 percent decreased this form of behavior over the school year. The program was also found to be effective with older kids in the fourth through seventh grades, as well as with kids who exhibited another type of aggression known as "relational aggression"—the kind that hurts others through gossiping, excluding others, and backstabbing.[2]

Gordon had this story about her program to share with *How to Change the World* author David Bornstein. A seventh-grade student in one of the Roots classes was attending a tough school in Toronto. Described as an effeminate boy from an immigrant background, the kid was inevitably, said Gordon, the butt of jokes. His comments in class unfailingly elicited rounds of snickers from the other boys.

One of the end-of-year tasks for kids in Roots is to write a poem or song for the baby. Most kids work in groups and come up with raps, but this particular boy decided to sing a song about mothers he'd written himself. "He was overweight and nerdy looking," Gordon recalled. "His social skills were not very good." Nervous about how the boy's classmates would respond, Gordon could only wait with bated breath. But they delivered, and nobly, too. No smirks. No snickers. Just the boy's due applause. "I was blown away," said Gordon, adding, "When they talk about protecting kids in schools, they talk about gun shields, cameras, lights, but never about the internal environment. But safe is not about the rules—it's about how the youngsters feel inside."

Bullies feed on power and play that dynamic very well. That's why when parents and educators respond to their actions by punishing them, they usually end up falling right into the bullies' hands. At the same time they lose the opportunity to make a longer-lasting impression about what it can feel like to be part of making someone feel bigger instead of smaller.

By holding off on responding to bullies with detentions or suspensions in favor of submerging them in experiences where they will be challenged to defend their aggressive behavior—not to someone else, but to themselves—school officials can break the cycle of aggression and punishment that wastes resources and dries up goodwill. A middle-school-age boy makes fun of a disabled classmate. Consider what might happen if, instead of working and eating alone for three days during an in-school suspension, he is asked to donate a couple of his lunch periods to help build handicap-accessible ramps for some of the school's outer buildings. What if he's asked to read to a small group of language-disabled kids in the elementary school? Here, the bully, who likely is accustomed to choosing social settings in which he can feel superior, is pressed to adapt to ones in which he cannot apply power in his customary ways. In these kinds of settings, the only way for him to gain respect from "bystanders" is by developing a new set of social skills (or dusting off an old set) and presenting himself in a more positive and pro-social light.

Speaking Up

It may indeed be human nature to jockey for position, make comparisons, seek out others' flaws, and create an inner and an outer group, but we still have a responsibility to protect others from our ungroomed thoughts. We have a responsibility to teach our children about being careful with theirs, too. While trying to accomplish this with platitudes about "respect" and "tolerance" won't get anyone very far, musing aloud about the difficulties inherent in being too tall, too short, too poor, too smart, too shy, too sad, or too loud stands a good chance of buying a person a little traction. And encouraging children toward performing small acts of kindness never gets old; my boys' father still tears up at his high school memory of having protected a mentally retarded boy from a lousy bunch of bullies.

Listen carefully to how your children talk and joke around with their friends. If you hear something objectionable, say something.

So you're making your car-pool rounds and hear your son make some joke to his friends about a kid in their class that ends with, *What does he care anyway, I don't think he's ever played a sport outside of gym class in his entire life!*

What do you do?

If you know the group of kids well, you can say something

like *Wow, I'm kind of surprised to hear you [to your son] say that, and kind of surprised that you guys all thought it was so funny.* Say it slowly and calmly so that the message doesn't get lost in an angry delivery that makes everyone uncomfortable and, in the future, wary of your presence. Your son most likely will respond with, *Mom, forget it, it was a joke, you don't need to take it so seriously . . .* And you can continue with, *Well, but it was a mean joke*—whereupon your son will likely cut you off with, *He wasn't even here . . .* So you say, *I don't think it matters whether he was here or not. I'm here, and it offends me. It should offend you.* If it doesn't feel too forced, you could go on with, *You're making fun of someone because he doesn't like to do the same things you guys like to do or that you guys think he should like to do. I think that's really old-fashioned thinking. I'm sorry, buddy, I don't mean to embarrass you and I don't mean to make you other guys uncomfortable. It just bothered me to hear something like that in my own car, so I needed to say something . . .*

And you just leave it there. The boys will be a little uncomfortable for a few more moments, but that's okay. The topic is stuck in the car, and they're stuck in the car with it. There's no need to drive any point home; you've already made it, and made it in a way they don't have to fight off.

Say you're a teacher walking down a school hallway. You come upon a couple of boys making jokes about another boy's poor catching skills. Go on over to them; a light "hey guys" let's them know you're not looking to reprimand them in public or yell. Ask them, curiously, *Why would you guys say something like that? Some people don't catch a ball well. That's such a big deal?* The boys will probably look at you guardedly, say nothing, and try to leave as quickly as possible.

But let's say one of the boys in the group says, *We were just kidding,* thinking he'll buy you off with that stock remark. And there it is—a beautiful window of opportunity to engage those couple of boys in a wisp of a conversation that lasts all of seven or eight seconds but drifts for even longer in their private thoughts. *Yeah, I figured you'd say that,* you say in response, *but I still don't get how it's funny to embarrass somebody or make him feel bad. We have so much fighting going on in this world, and so many people already feel bad. Why not do something to make them feel better?* And then you shrug and walk away, leaving the boys to have to exit the topic on their own, since you left them with it still out there on the table in front of them all.

"Unpack" the language surrounding the word *boy,* so it means only that—a boy—and doesn't include all the stereotypical and unappealing traits that supposedly go with being a boy, e.g., being inattentive, aggressive, mischievous, or thoroughly disinterested in social "niceties." Resist the definition of boys as necessarily sports loving, or aggressive, or insensitive.

On a playground in Abu Dhabi, Beth watches a ten-year-old boy standing by a water fountain, spraying just himself—and anyone walking by. An adult passerby says, "He's such a boy." A few minutes later, Beth sees another boy walk over to the fountain and punch the boy who has been playing. In response, someone else says, similarly, "Boys will be boys."

This simple phrase has served as an inadvertent disguise for male bad behavior for too long. Boys *will* do things that most girls won't—tackle their younger brother onto the couch for fun, blow snot rockets in the shower, and leave the house without brushing their teeth—but the difference between gender-influenced behavior that is fun or funny (or just gross), and behavior that purposely annoys, offends, or hurts other people, is huge. Over time, and reinforced by culturally sanctioned gender norms, the term *boy* has come to define not only a young male person but also a *state of behavior.* In small but recognizable ways, it absolves males of the responsibility to be accountable for the impact of their behavior on the people around them. Boys who hurt are not being boys—they are being bullies. However by "unpacking" the language, and refusing to tolerate behavior just because it has been described as coming from boys, we can take the necessary steps toward reinstating levels of personal accountability that are instrumental in the social and emotional development of self-respecting, kind, dignified young boys and men. These will be the good citizens of family and community and the globe that we all—collectively and individually—need, and can be proud to have raised.

POSTSCRIPT

Jake and his twin brother, Austin, are sixteen years old now. Casey is nineteen, and away at college. We've all lived with this book in the making for seven years. I had worried that once they got older, and thought about what it meant to be in a book written by their mother, of all people, they would ask to be written out of it, or at least somewhat disguised. But it turned out they wanted nothing changed, and needed nothing removed.

I know Jake really appreciated my idea for this book, and even more that I followed through on writing it. From a personal perspective, the timing couldn't have been worse; there was enormous upheaval in my life, plus the loss of my father and brother. I was determined, though, not to let those things take the book down. In addition, soon after agreeing to join me in writing this book, Beth moved to Abu Dhabi, in the United Arab Emirates, in order to be with her architect husband who was employed there. As another mother of three boys, and as someone passionate about the need to be talking with all our children about the role of citizenship in building healthier communities, and by extension, in building healthier, more compassionate citizens, Beth, too, did her share to keep this project moving forward.

There was, however, one thing Beth and I never managed to figure out while writing this book: a good alternative for the term *nonathletic*. Nonathletic as the obverse of athletic implies that athleticism is the norm. This is akin to calling someone who is not intellectually gifted "nonintelligent." We refer to good musicians or artists or linguists as being talented; everyone else is just considered "normal." In general, people aren't expected to be innately good at those things. It's just nice when it happens.

But there was just no other suitable word or phrase for "boys who don't like sports." And so, they were called "boys who don't like sports," or "those boys," and on occasion, because it kept a sentence from getting too wordy, "nonathletic." But come to think of it, we don't have other expressions or words for nonmusical or nonartistic, and it's probably because we don't need them. Most people don't expect to be born so inclined, so they're not offended by the prefix. It just goes to show the degree to which being athletic is packaged with being a boy.

Oh well. Maybe there are more important tasks at hand. Like making sure these boys have our collective attention, for instance. Like making sure someone is talking to them and on behalf of them, and validating the importance of their contributions. Making sure that people take their social marginalization from the core cluster of kids seriously, rather than viewing it as just another "phase" of childhood. Making sure that people are stepping in to stop ugly behavior among all children, whenever it's witnessed. Making sure that these boys are given opportunities to have voices in the community and that, over time, they feel empowered to begin making their own.

One very important takeaway from *The Last Boys Picked* is this: that just because a boy doesn't fit in with the hegemonic world of sporty boys doesn't mean he won't fit in someplace else. "There are other ways for boys to determine their self-worth, their purpose, and the places they belong," Bill Bryan once said to me. "But they do have to go out and find them."

Jake is finding his places. He's one of those come-from-behinders, the kid who matures in the shadows and then surprises everyone with the scope of his intelligence and sharp wit. Coolheaded and unflinching in the face of calamity or pandemonium, Jake is becoming a pillar of measured composure.

We find signs that our kids are okay in a variety of places, often through serendipity. One day I drove Jake and a friend to school—a boy similarly not keen on playing sports. The three of us had been talking about the book, and I asked the friend how he felt about being one of those boys who didn't care too much for sports. Easily and brightly, the boy replied, "Well, we're not considered popular, but we have a lot of friends." And with that, he and Jake hopped out of the car and strode into school.

Janet Sasson Edgette

ACKNOWLEDGMENTS

Janet:

Many thanks to agents Jane Dystel and Miriam Goderich, who encouraged me to tackle this subject, and to write a 'bigger' book. Thank you, too, Chasya Milgram, Stephanie deVita, Morris Shamah, and Rachel Stout, for helping to guide this project to its fruition. Tremendous thanks to Denise Silvestro at Berkley Books for her belief in the merit of a book about excluded boys, and, along with assistant Meredith Giordan, for the valuable editorial guidance.

Thank you to my sister, Carol Sasson, without whose support, humor, and encouragement I'd not have been able to rally as I did over the last five years past the overwhelming tumult in my life. You made it possible for me to be at peace with what was behind me, and expectant about what was to come. And I considered it a gift to have you with me as we said goodbye together to the men in our own family—our father, our brother.

Thank you to my three boys, Casey, Austin, and Jake: you guys are attentive and kind and very funny. You were each so generous with your selves and your time at a point in our lives when you rightfully could have insisted on having more of mine. Because this book was so important to me, you all let me know that it had become important to you.

Bill Bryan—one of those last boys picked—you were an invaluable resource. Your vivid stories and discerning observations contributed greatly to the book, and reinforced the importance of it getting written. Thank you.

Thank you to Dr. Glenn Paskow, and to the other boys and men who gave their stories.

Thank you to psychologist Dr. Bonnie Socket, for your assistance with the subject of learning disabilities.

Thank you so much Mary Beth Wiig, who I know as Bert, and Andrea Lovett, who saw me through some rather trying moments, and upon whose lofty hearts and strong shoulders and musical gifts I was able to carry on.

Thank you, too, Noreen Vigilante and Mary Ellen Myers, for your kind and generous attention and support, for your help with rides and painting and casseroles. You taught me a lot about the value of community.

To all the baseball moms and dads and friends, who were instrumental in making sure Austin got to all those games and tournaments, and back home again—thank you.

And, finally, to my coauthor and colleague and dear friend,

Beth—I offer countless thanks. You made this a better and bigger book, one that became more than a book about the boy who gets picked last. You helped it become also a book about the communities in which these boys are raised, and about how these communities can build belonging instead of tolerating exclusion. And you were the author of one of our most central points—that all of us lose out when we allow even one of us to be left out. You took ideas of mine and blew them up and out—like one of those exploded-view diagrams—and together we filled in the new spaces. Please come back home soon.

Beth:

As we each find our support and inspiration in different places, I want to thank those who helped me be a better mother, wife, educator, and contributor to this book, beginning with my sons Alexander, Nathan, and Ethan. Each of you know me at my best and worst and continue loving me and each other. Thank you. I am proud to be your mother; you will each make a wonderful partner in life and love.

I share Janet's thanks to all of the people who worked with us to bring this book to fruition.

Thanks and gratitude to:

Dodi Li Klimoff, a friend of a lifetime. Beth Razin my "phone a friend"—you know more than most people ever learn. Margery and Chris Comer Payne, my readers. Heather Margolis Warner, my sister, who continues having brilliant ideas on the way the world should be. Annie and Susan, my friends who always tell me how to spell, that I have greens in my teeth, and my thinking is on point, or not, I trust you. All of my students and leaders from the Satell Fellowship, who challenge the systems, fight for justice, and contribute your time in service. To colleagues, Ari Goldberg and Regina Black Lennox from Gratz College, Mark Thourburn and Jini Loos at The Haverford School, and James Jerry Clark, diversity educator. Nicolas, a young man brave enough to share his life stories, Christine Kodman-Jones, Ph.D., who helped me understand my children and my mothering. My parents and grandparents who provided me with a sense of heritage, faith and courage to love my friends and family unconditionally. All of you are mirrors, reflections of the world around and provide a true image of what is inside and out. I am grateful beyond words.

To Dr. Jane Goodall, Roots & Shoots founder and visionary who set the example for how to live and contribute for a better world.

Mostly, thank you Janet—you are the driving force, a force of nature who makes thoughts and words a reality. Now all we need is to take the words on these pages and construct a new stage for all boys.

You all give me hope.

NOTES

CHAPTER ONE

1 Amy Dickinson, "Bad Boys Rule," *Time*, January 31, 2000.

2 "Playground Politics: Lack of Athletic Skill Often Means Loneliness and Peer Rejection," *Science Daily: News and Articles in Science, Health, Environment and Technology*, October 2007, accessed June 5, 2010, http://www.sciencedaily .com/releases/2007/10/071019085951.htm.

3 "Bullying Widespread in U.S. Schools, Survey Finds," the Eunice Kennedy Shriver National Institute of Child Health and Human Development Official Home Page, http://www.nichd.nih.gov/news/releases/bullying.cfm.

CHAPTER TWO

1 Laurie Helgoe, "Revenge of the Introvert," *Psychology Today*, September/ October 2010, 54.

2 Bonnie Golden, *Self-Esteem and Psychological Type: Definitions, Interactions and Expressions*. CAPT, Florida: 1994.

3 M. Miyahara, "Developmental Dyspraxia and Developmental Coordination Disorder," *Neuropsychology Review* 4 (December 5, 1995), 245–268.

Madeleine M. Portwood, *Understanding Developmental Dyspraxia: A Textbook for Students and Professionals* (London: David Fulton, 2001).

4 "Visual Processing Disorder and Dyslexia," Behavioural Neurotherapy Clinic, accessed March 2, 2012, http://www.adhd.com.au/Visual_Processing_Dis orders.htm.

5 Kids Can Do Children's Therapy Center, www.kidscando.org/sensory_integration.html.

6 Phil Sheridan, "Storybook Ending in Weir's Sights," *Philadelphia Inquirer,* February 15, 2006, E7.

CHAPTER THREE

1 George Walter Fiske, *Boy Life and Self-Government.* (New York: Young Men's Christian Association Press, 1912).

2 E. Anthony Rotundo, *American Manhood: Transformations in Masculinity from the Revolution to the Modern Era* (New York: Basic Books, 1993).

3 Bessie Z., "Student Athletes—'Model' Athletes?," *Teen Ink,* n.d., http://www.teenink.com/opinion/all/article/9906/Student-Athletes—ldquoModelrdquo Adolescents/.

4 "Jockocracy," Urban Dictionary, accessed March 2, 2012, http://www.urban dictionary.com/define.php?term=jockocracy.

5 "Jock Privilege," *Teaching Tolerance: A Project of the Southern Poverty Law Center,* n.d., http://www.teachingtolerance.org/supplement/jock-privilege.

6 Ibid.

7 Ibid.

8 Barbara Kerr, "Gender and Genius," Keynote speech delivered at the National Curriculum Networking Conference, the College of William and Mary, Williamsburg, VA, March 1, 2000, http://www.megt.org.

9 Barbara A. Kerr and Megan Foley Nicpon, "Gender and Giftedness," in N. Colangelo and G. A. Davis, eds., *Handbook of Gifted Education,* 3rd Edition (Boston: Allyn and Bacon, 2003), 493–505.

10 J. A. Wolfle, "Underachieving Gifted Males: Are We Missing the Boat?" *Roeper Review* 13 (1991), 181–184.

11 Dawn E. Warden, "College Bound (and Worried)," *Main Life Today,* September 2008, accessed November 2008, http://www.mainlinetoday.com/Main -Line-Today/September-2008/College-Bound-and-Worried/.

12 "Personal Best," *Teaching Tolerance: A Project of the Southern Poverty Law Center,* Fall 2002, http://www.tolerance.org/magazine/number-22-fall-2002/personal-best.

CHAPTER FIVE

1 The four basic stereotyped male ideals: the "sturdy oak," "give 'em hell," the "big wheel," "no sissy stuff." Deborah S. David and Robert Brannon, *The Forty-Nine Percent Majority: The Male Sex Role* (Reading, MA: Addison-Wesley, 1976).

CHAPTER SIX

1 Carrie Rickey, "A Metrosexual Meets a Caveman," *Philadelphia Inquirer*, March 20, 2009, W4, W16.

2 "Gender: Getting Beyond the Differences," accessed January 9, 2012, http://webspace.webring.com/people/uu/um_2216/gender2.html.

3 National Football League, *Teaching Tolerance: A Project of the Southern Poverty Law Center*, accessed May 2011, http://www.tolerance.org/activity/reducing-gender-stereotyping-and-homophobia-sports.

4 Kelly Whiteside, "U.S. Men Shut Out; Plushenko Has His Day," *USA Today*, February 17, 2006, 3F.

5 "Michael Madsen's Fatherly Advice." *Men's Health*, February 21, 2004. Accessed March 3, 2008. http://www.menshealth.com/men/best-life/family-guy/michael-madsens-fatherly-advice/.

6 David D. Gilmore, *Manhood in the Making: Cultural Concepts of Masculinity.* (New Haven, CT: Yale University, 1990), 177.

CHAPTER SEVEN

1 "Mister Rogers defending PBS to the US Senate." (Fred Rogers's 1969 appearance before the United States Senate Subcommittee on Communications), YouTube, accessed February 2008. http://www.youtube.com/watch?v=yXEuEUQIP3Q.

2 Tom Junod, "Fred Rogers," http://en.goldenmap.com/Fred_Rogers.

3 Quoted in Joel Stein, "Can Obama Overcome the Urkel Effect?," *Time*, October 31, 2008.

4 Cardinal John Henry Newman, "The Idea of a University," cited in Waller R. Newell, ed., *What Is a Man?: 3,000 Years of Wisdom on the Art of Manly Virtue* (New York: HarperCollins, 2000), in his intro to the chapter "The Gentleman."

5 Cynthia Hubert, "Men, Even the Manliest, Are Embracing the Hug," *Philadelphia Inquirer*, March 11, 2007, 6.

6 Ibid.

7 Tim Stack, "Chris Colfer Makes Some Noise," *Entertainment Weekly*, November 12, 2010, 48.

8 James T. Webb, Elizabeth A. Meckstroth, and Stephanie S. Tolan, *Guiding the Gifted Child: A Practical Source for Parents and Teachers* (Scottsdale, AZ: Great Potential Press, 1989).

CHAPTER NINE

1 "Harvey C. Mansfield on Manliness," Peter Schramm's "You Americans," podcast, March 8, 2006, http://www.ashbrook.org/podcasts/schramm/06-03-08_mansfield.mp3.

2 "Witnesses to Bullying May Face More Mental Health Risks Than Bullies and Victims." *Science Daily*, December 14, 2009, http://www.sciencedaily.com/releases/2009/12/091214121449.htm.

3 "The Role of Bullies, Victims, and Witnesses," the ABC's of Bullying: Addressing, Blocking, and Curbing School Aggression, CSAP's Prevention Pathways: Online Courses, http://pathwayscourses.samhsa.gov/bully/bully_2_pg12.htm.

4 Ibid.

5 Kaethe Weingarten. *Common Shock: Witnessing Violence Every Day* (New York: Dutton, 2003).

6 Thank you to Dr. Fred Levine, former professor, Hahnemann University graduate psychology program, for this story.

7 Steven Rea, "Not So Beautiful," *Philadelphia Inquirer*, February 1, 2011, C1, C5.

8 Kathleen O'Toole, "The Stanford Prison Experiment: Still Powerful after All These Years," *Stanford News*, January 8, 1997.

CHAPTER TEN

1 Debby A. Phillips, "Reproducing Normative and Marginalized Masculinities: Adolescent Male Popularity and the Outcast," *Nursing Inquiry* 12:3 (2005), doi:10.1111/j.1440-1800.2005.00271.x.

2 David Bornstein, "Fighting Bullying with Babies," *New York Times*, November 8, 2010, accessed January 1, 2011, http://opinionator.blogs.nytimes.com/2010/11/08/fighting-bullying-with-babies/?ref=cyberbullying.

BIBLIOGRAPHY

Alexander, Duane. "Bullying Widespread in U.S. Schools, Survey Finds." NICHD, the Eunice Kennedy Shriver National Institute of Child Health and Human Development Official Home Page, accessed December 15, 2011.

Armstrong, Jennifer. "Gay Teens on TV." *Entertainment Weekly,* January 28, 2011.

Bornstein, David. "Fighting Bullying with Babies." *New York Times,* November 8, 2010.

Burling, Stacey. "Swimmer Remembered as a Generous Spirit." *Philadelphia Inquirer,* October 31, 2010.

Carey, Art. "The Meaning of Manly." *Philadelphia Inquirer,* April 8, 2006.

Children's Vision Information Network. "Reading and Vision." http://www.child rensvision.com/reading.htm, accessed January 6, 2012.

Collins, James C., and Jerry I. Porras. *Built to Last: Successful Habits of Visionary Companies.* New York: HarperBusiness, 2004.

Corbett, Ken. *Boyhoods: Rethinking Masculinities.* New Haven: Yale University Press, 2009.

Cross, Gary S. *Men to Boys: The Making of Modern Immaturity.* New York: Columbia University Press, 2008.

David, Deborah S., and Robert Brannon. *The Forty-nine Percent Majority: The Male Sex Role.* Reading, MA: Addison-Wesley, 1976.

Diagnostic and Statistical Manual of Mental Disorders: DSM-IV-TR, 4th Edition. Washington, D.C.: American Psychiatric Association, 2000.

Dickinson, Amy. "Bad Boys Rule." *Time,* January 31, 2000.

Dunow, Henry. *The Way Home: Scenes from a Season, Lessons from a Lifetime.* New York: Broadway Books, 2001.

Fiske, George Walter. *Boy Life and Self-Government.* New York: Young Men's Christian Association Press, 1912.

Fitzpatrick, Frank. "For Weir, Bad Day Has No Silver Lining." *Philadelphia Inquirer,* February 17, 2006.

Garcia, Guy. *Decline of Men: How the American Male Is Tuning Out, Giving Up, and Flipping Off His Future.* New York: HarperCollins, 2008.

Gilmore, David D. *Manhood in the Making: Cultural Concepts of Masculinity.* New Haven: Yale University Press, 1990.

Golden, Bonnie. *Self-Esteem and Psychological Type: Definitions, Interactions and Expressions.* CAPT, Florida: 1994.

Golding, William. *Lord of the Flies: a Novel.* New York: Berkley Publishing Group, 1960.

Gould, Jason. "The Price of a Beer in Boston." *The Martial Musings of an Artist of Life* (web log), June 22, 2007. http://jasongould.blogspot.com/2007/06/price-of-beer-in-boston.html, accessed January 6, 2012.

Greenspan, Stanley. *Playground Politics: Understanding the Emotional Life of Your School-Aged Child.* Cambridge, MA: Da Capo Press, 1994.

Gurian, Michael. *A Fine Young Man: What Parents, Mentors and Educators Can Do to Shape Adolescent Boys into Exceptional Men.* New York: Tarcher, 1998.

Gurian, Michael. *The Wonder of Boys: What Parents, Mentors and Educators Can Do to Shape Boys into Exceptional Men.* New York: Tarcher, 2006.

Harris, Judith Rich. *The Nurture Assumption: Why Children Turn Out the Way They Do.* New York: Free Press, 1998.

Helgoe, Laurie. "Revenge of the Introvert" *Psychology Today,* September/October 2010, 54.

Hubert, Cynthia. "Men, Even the Manliest, Are Embracing the Hug." *Philadelphia Inquirer,* March 11, 2007.

Hymowitz, Kay S. *Ready or Not: What Happens When We Treat Children as Small Adults.* San Francisco: Encounter Books, 2000.

John-Hall, Annette. "Manly Men Can Wear Cleats and Dance Shoes." *Philadelphia Inquirer,* August 30, 2006.

Junod, Tom. Excerpt from *Esquire.* http://www.pittsburghinwords.org/tom_junod .html, accessed January 2009.

Kadaba, Lini S. and Elizabeth Wellington. "Manning Up; as the Testosterone Turns: The New Retrosexual Gets That Strong and Gallant Guy Thing Going Again." *Philadelphia Inquirer,* March 7, 2010.

Kerr, Barbara. "Gender and Genius." Keynote speech delivered at the National Curriculum Networking Conference, the College of William and Mary, Williamsburg, VA, March 1, 2000. http://cfge.wm.edu/documents/GenderGenius.htm, accessed March 4, 2007.

———. *Smart Girls Two: A New Psychology of Girls, Women, and Giftedness.* Dayton, OH: Ohio Psychology Press, 1994.

——— *Smart Girls, Gifted Women.* Columbus, OH: Ohio Psychology Publications, 1985.

Kerr, Barbara A., and Sanford J. Cohn. *Smart Boys: Talent, Manhood, and the Search for Meaning.* Scottsdale, AZ: Gifted Potential Press, 2001.

Kerr, B. A., and M. Foley Nicpon. "Gender and Giftedness." In N. Colangelo and G. A. Davis, eds., *Handbook of Gifted Education,* 3rd Edition. Boston, MA: Allyn and Bacon.

Kids Can Do, Inc. Children's Therapy Center. "Sensory Integration: An Overview." Sensory Integration in Children's Therapy. April 4, 2006. http://www.kidscando .org/sensory_integration.html.

Kimmel, Michael S. *The Gendered Society.* New York: Oxford University Press, 2008.

Kindlon, Daniel J., Michael Thompson, and Teresa Barker. *Raising Cain: Protecting the Emotional Life of Boys.* New York: Ballantine Books, 1999.

Kranowitz, Carol Stock. *The Out-of-Sync Child: Recognizing and Coping with Sensory Integration Dysfunction.* New York: Perigee Books, 1998.

Kutscher, Martin L., Tony Attwood, and Robert R. Wolff. *Kids in the Syndrome Mix of ADHD, LD, Asperger's, Tourette's, Bipolar and More!: The One Stop Guide for Parents, Teachers, and Other Professionals.* London: Jessica Kingsley, 2005.

Laney, Marti Olsen. *The Hidden Gifts of the Introverted Child: Helping Your Child Thrive in an Extroverted World.* New York: Workman Publishing Company, 2005.

Leo, John. "Parent-free Zone." *U.S. News & World Report,* November 1, 1999.

LeShan, Lawrence L. *The Dilemma of Psychology: A Psychologist Looks at His Troubled Profession*. New York: Dutton, 1990.

Lifton, Robert Jay. *The Protean Self: Human Resilience in an Age of Fragmentation*. Chicago, IL: University of Chicago Press, 1999.

Louv, Richard. *Last Child in the Woods: Saving Our Children from Nature-Deficit Disorder*. Chapel Hill, NC: Algonquin Books of Chapel Hill, 2005.

Madsen, Michael. "Michael Madsen's Fatherly Advice." *Men's Health,* February 21, 2004.

Mansfield, Harvey C. *Manliness*. New Haven: Yale University Press, 2006.

Marget, Kathryn. "2008 MEGT Position Paper Explores Underachievement Among Gifted Boys." *Newsletter of the Metro Chapter of the Minnesota Educators of the Gifted and Talented,* Fall 2008. www.megt.org, http://www.megt.org/links/2008%20PDF%20FINAL%20MEGT%20newsletter%20FALL.pdf.

Marinoff, Lou. *Plato, Not Prozac!: Applying Eternal Wisdom to Everyday Problems*. New York: HarperCollins, 1999.

McKay, Brett, and Kate McKay. *The Art of Manliness: Classic Skills and Manners for the Modern Man*. Cincinnati: HOW Books, 2009.

Messner, Michael. "Boyhood, Organized Sports, and the Construction Of Masculinities." *Journal of Contemporary Ethnography* 18:4 (1990): 416–444. doi:10.1177/089124190018004003.

Mirman, David. "Crisis of Modern American Masculinity." Carnegie Mellon University. http://www.andrew.cmu.edu.

Myers, Isabel Briggs with Peter Myers. *Gifts Differing*. California: Consulting Psychological Press, 1995.

Neal, Mark Anthony. *New Black Man*. New York: Routledge, 2006.

Newell, Waller R., ed. *What Is a Man?: 3,000 Years of Wisdom on the Art of Manly Virtue*. New York: HarperCollins, 2000.

Nikkah, John, and Leah Furman. *Our Boys Speak: Adolescent Boys Write About Their Inner Lives*. New York: St. Martin's Griffin, 2000.

"NINDS Learning Disabilities Information Page." National Institute of Neurological Disorders and Stroke. http://www.ninds.nih.gov/disorders/learningdisabilities/learningdisabilities.htm.

"Nonverbal Learning Disorders." *Education News,* July 28, 2008. http://www.educationnews.org/articles/27710/1/Nonverbal-learning-disorders-NLD/Page1.html.

O'Toole, Kathleen. "The Stanford Prison Experiment: Still Powerful After All These Years." *Stanford News,* January 8, 1997.

Pathways Courses. "Addressing, Blocking, and Curbing School Aggression." The ABCs of Bullying. http://pathwayscourses.samhsa.gov/courses.htm.

Phillips, Debby A. "Reproducing Normative and Marginalized Masculinities: Adolescent Male Popularity and the Outcast." *Nursing Inquiry* 12:3 (2005), 219–230. doi:10.1111/j.1440-1800.2005.00271.x.

Pierangelo, Roger, and George A. Giuliani. "Prevalence of Learning Disabilities." *Learning Disabilities: A Practical Approach to Foundations, Assessment, Diagnosis, and Teaching.* New York: Merrill, 2006.

Pollack, William S. *Real Boys: Rescuing Our Sons from the Myths of Boyhood.* New York: Henry Holt, 1998.

Portwood, Madeleine M. *Understanding Developmental Dyspraxia: A Textbook for Students and Professionals.* London: David Fulton, 2001.

Rao, Anthony, and Michelle D. Seaton. *The Way of Boys: Raising Healthy Boys in a Challenging and Complex World.* New York: William Morrow, 2009.

Rea, Steven. "Not So Beautiful." *Philadelphia Inquirer,* February 1, 2011.

"Reading and Vision." Children's Vision Information Network. http://www.childrensvision.com/reading.htm, accessed April 2011.

Rickey, Carrie. "A Metrosexual Meets a Caveman." *Philadelphia Inquirer,* March 20, 2009.

Rivers, Ian, V. Paul Poteat, Nathalie Noret, Nigel Ashurst. "Observing Bullying at School: The Mental Health Implications of Witness Status." *School Psychology Quarterly* 24:4 (2009): 211–213. doi:10.1037/a0018164.

Rotundo, E. Anthony. *American Manhood: Transformations in Masculinity from the Revolution to the Modern Era.* New York: Basic Books, 1993.

Science Daily. News and Articles in Science, Health, Environment, and Technology. "Playground Politics: Lack of Athletic Skill Often Means Loneliness and Peer Rejection." October 2007. http://www.sciencedaily.com/releases/2007/10/071019085951.htm, accessed June 5, 2010.

Science Daily. News and Articles in Science, Health, Environment, and Technology. "Witnesses to Bullying May Face More Mental Health Risks Than Bullies and Victims." December 14, 2009. http://www.sciencedaily.com/releases/2009/12/091214121449.htm.

"Sensory Integration—An Overview." Kids Can Do, Inc., Children's Therapy Center. Sensory Integration in Children's Therapy. Accessed April 4, 2006. http:// kidscando.org/sensory_integration.html.

Sheridan, Phil. "Weir's Sizzle Fizzles." *Philadelphia Inquirer,* February 17, 2006.

———. "Storybook Ending in Weir's Sights." *Philadelphia Inquirer,* February 15, 2006.

Sidanius, Jim, and Felicia Pratto. *Social Dominance.* Cambridge, U.K.: Cambridge University Press, 1999.

Sommers, Christina Hoff. *The War Against Boys: How Misguided Feminism Is Harming Our Young Men.* New York: Simon and Schuster, 2000.

Spiegelman, Willard. *Seven Pleasures: Essays on Ordinary Happiness.* New York: Farrar, Straus and Giroux, 2009.

Stack, Tim. "Chris Colfer Makes Some Noise." *Entertainment Weekly,* November 12, 2010.

Starr, Mark. "Coach, Teacher, Believer." *Newsweek,* July 16, 2007.

Stein, Joel. "The Urkel Effect: Barack Obama May Conquer Racial Prejudice, but Can He Beat Back America's Nerdophobia." *Time,* November 10, 2008.

Stockdale, Carol, and Carol Possin. "New Horizons for Learning: Spatial Relations and Learning." *Johns Hopkins University School of Education.* http://education .jhu.edu/newhorizons#ark, accessed May 2011.

Tannen, Deborah. *You Just Don't Understand: Women and Men in Conversation.* New York: Ballantine Books, 1990.

Teaching Tolerance: A Project of the Southern Poverty Law Center. "Jock Privilege." www .teachingtolerance.org/supplement/jock-privilege, accessed January 6, 2012.

———. "Personal Best." Fall 2002. http://www.tolerance.org/magazine/ number-22-fall-2002/personal-best.

Vincent, Norah. *Self-Made Man: One Woman's Journey into Manhood and Back Again.* New York: Viking, 2006.

"Visual Processing and Dyslexia." Behavioral Neurotherapy Clinic. http://www .adhd.com.au/Visual_Processing_Disorders.htm, accessed April 2011.

Von Drehle, David. "The Boys Are All Right." *Time,* August 6, 2007.

Warden, Dawn E. "College Bound (and Worried)." *Main Life Today,* September 2008.

Webb, James T., Elizabeth A. Meckstroth, and Stephanie S. Tolan. *Guiding the Gifted Child: A Practical Source for Parents and Teachers.* Scottdale, AZ: Great Potential Press, 1989.

Weingarten, Kaethe. *Common Shock: Witnessing Violence Every Day.* New York: Dutton, 2003.

West, Cornel. "The Moral Obligations of Living in a Democratic Society." In David Batstone and Eduardo Mendieta. eds. *The Good Citizen.* New York: Routledge, 1998.

"What Is Dyspraxia?" National Center for Learning Disabilities. http://www.ncld.org/ld-basics/ld-aamp-language/writing/dyspraxia.

Whiteside, Kelly. "U.S. Men Shut Out; Plushenko Has His Day." *USA Today,* February 17, 2006.

Wolfle, J. A. "Underachieving Gifted Males: Are We Missing the Boat?" *Roeper Review* 13 (1991).

Wortel, Avi. *S.O.R. Losers.* Scarsdale, NY: Bradbury Press, 1984.

YouTube. "Mr. Rogers Defending PBS to the US Senate." Fred Rogers's 1969 appearance before the United States Senate Subcommittee on Communications. http://www.youtube.com/watch?v=yXEuEUQIP3Q, accessed February 2008.